**Piano*Trainer* Series**

# The Advanced Pianist Book 2

A technical and musical curriculum
for pianists at Grade 7–8 level

**Karen Marshall**
and Mark Tanner as the Concert Pianist

**FABER *ff* MUSIC**

# Contents

Dedicated to my wise and loving teacher, the late Enid Oughtibridge, with whom I completed my Grade 8 back in 1991. Also to all the students who have studied advanced piano with me over several decades. You have all guided me enormously in the writing of this book. Thank you for your inspiration, dedication and for making my job as a teacher such a joy.

Special mention must be given to the following friends and colleagues for their support and help in writing these books: Kathryn Page, David Barton, Andrew Eales, Gareth Green, Heather Hammond, Rowan Cozens, Penny Stirling and Gily Poznansky. Huge thanks also to my family, my husband Adam, son Jacob and two daughters, Anna and Naomi. All have played their part in scanning proofs, commenting on piece selection and giving me the time and support to get the work done!

© 2019 by Faber Music Ltd
This edition first published in 2019
Bloomsbury House, 74–77 Great Russell Street, London WC1B 3DA
Music processed by Jackie Leigh
Text designed by Susan Clarke
Cover design by Adam Hay
Printed in England by Caligraving Ltd
All rights reserved

ISBN10: 0-571-54117-8
EAN13: 978-0-571-54117-1

To buy Faber Music publications or to find out about the full range of titles available please contact your local music retailer or Faber Music sales enquiries:
Faber Music Ltd, Burnt Mill, Elizabeth Way, Harlow CM20 2HX
Tel: +44 (0) 1279 82 89 82   Fax: +44 (0) 1279 82 89 83
sales@fabermusic.com   fabermusicstore.com

# Introduction

*The Advanced Pianist* books 1 and 2 complete the PianoTrainer series. They have been written with the express aim of empowering developing pianists to truly understand and interpret the music they are playing and provide material that gives a musical and technical foundation for advanced repertoire – Grade 6 and beyond.

This book includes five chapters that can be studied over several months. Each chapter explores a different musical period through a variety of elements, including historical and musical context and a range of repertoire by a featured composer. There's also an exciting section called 'Concert pianist', which provides advanced playing tips and wise commentary from the pianist, Mark Tanner. Each chapter contains a variety of elements as described below. The music deliberately spans a range of difficulty levels, so some pieces can be learnt in just one or two weeks, whilst others are more challenging.

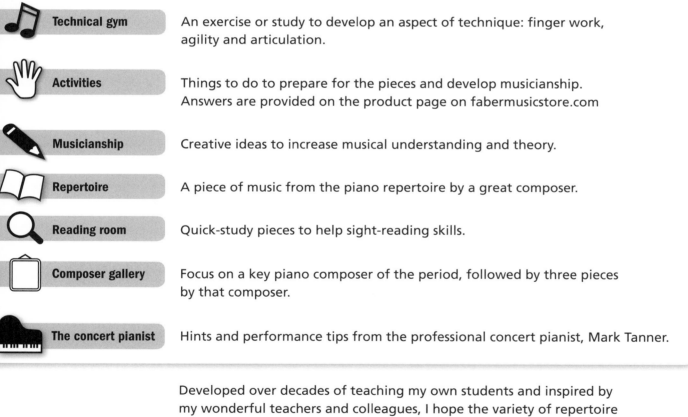

**Technical gym**  An exercise or study to develop an aspect of technique: finger work, agility and articulation.

**Activities**  Things to do to prepare for the pieces and develop musicianship. Answers are provided on the product page on fabermusicstore.com

**Musicianship**  Creative ideas to increase musical understanding and theory.

**Repertoire**  A piece of music from the piano repertoire by a great composer.

**Reading room**  Quick-study pieces to help sight-reading skills.

**Composer gallery**  Focus on a key piano composer of the period, followed by three pieces by that composer.

**The concert pianist**  Hints and performance tips from the professional concert pianist, Mark Tanner.

Developed over decades of teaching my own students and inspired by my wonderful teachers and colleagues, I hope the variety of repertoire and pedagogical content in this book will provide great enjoyment to all pianists – young people, adult returners and even piano teachers! I must also acknowledge Mark Tanner and our editor, Lesley Rutherford, for their outstanding contributions to the books.

Karen Marshall

Please note the repertoire included in *The Advanced Pianist* books aims to support students and teachers as clearly and simply as possible, so does include editorial changes and additions to original editions. The pieces have been grouped loosely into musical periods but inevitably some overlaps have occurred. Technical, Musicianship and Reading room pieces are not necessarily of the period of the chapter.

### Early keyboard instruments

Renaissance keyboard music (ca 1400–1600) was written for the organ, virginal and clavichord. Whilst the clavichord continued to be popular in the Baroque period, the virginal gave way to larger keyboards: the spinet and harpsichord.

The concert pianist

### Baroque keyboards

The generic term 'clavier' is a helpful collective noun for the various keyboards of the Baroque era (1600–1750). Each instrument has its own distinctive timbre and feel: a plucking mechanism for the harpsichord, and a striking action for the clavichord.

### Touch and articulation

The physical characteristics of Baroque instruments impact on their tone, projection and duration. Compared with the modern piano, their smaller dimensions, wooden frames and light feel under the fingers led to a more intimate, articulation-based mode of delivery requiring the subtlest of touches.

### Phrasing

Phrasing, and in particular dynamics, need to be weighed up in light of the small physical form of these instruments and their short sustain. In contrast with the plucked variety, the clavichord could bring a degree of note-by-note dynamic shading into play (even vibrato and portamento), though such effects are delicately nuanced compared with the modern, iron-framed piano.

### Rhythm and metre

A clear sense of pulse is of utmost importance when playing early music. Subtle variations in tempo and articulation made a world of difference to 18th-century players, and ornaments were invaluable too. Besides adding brilliance, ornaments gave an illusion of a sustained note. Melodies were often vocally conceived, hence profit from the kinds of expression and rubato a singer might introduce.

### Tone production

The dynamic range we enjoy today would have bewildered a Baroque keyboard player. But rather than behaving 'politely' when interpreting this music, we should keep contrapuntal textures crystal clear, different voice entries audible and moments of harmonic tension and release carefully emphasised.

### Use of pedals

Though the sustain pedal did not exist on early keyboards, tasteful use may assist pianists when connecting tricky intervals or adding a little bloom to chords at cadences. Una corda is best left out of the equation.

Listen to these works of different genres from the Renaissance and Baroque periods.
- **Orchestral** Overtures by Jean-Philippe Rameau
- **Chamber or solo** Cello Suites by J.S. Bach
- **Choral** *Gloria* by Antonio Vivaldi

The following repertoire is recommended for performance or study:
- *Passacaglia* from Suite No.6 in G minor by G.F. Handel
- *Little Preludes*, *Two-Part Inventions* and Allemande from *Partita No.1 in B♭ major* by J.S. Bach
- Sonata in E major K.380 by Scarlatti
- *Italian Concerto*, Allegro, by J.S. Bach

This piece is entirely based on broken chords and scales, moving quickly through hand position changes. Choreograph these by playing them as chords first, and mark in your fingerings. Try to practise all the possible arpeggio patterns regularly:

* All the major and minor keys in root position, first and second inversions.
* Broken chords in triads (C E G, E G C, etc.)
* Broken chords in full, with the tonic at the top and bottom (C E G C, E G C E, etc.)
* Diminished 7ths and dominant 7ths in root position and inversions.

## Little Fantasy

C.P.E. Bach
(1714–1788)

🎹 **Concert pianist**

For ascending arpeggios and broken chords, the thumb should guide the hand into each new position as early as possible, with a minimum of up/down wrist motion or circular elbow movement to avoid unwanted bumps. Enjoy how it feels to cover each new triad fractionally ahead of actually playing the notes. Practising triads as a succession of block chords can be useful, too. Obviously broken chords use the thumb more frequently than arpeggios, so keeping a light, curved hand close to the keys will help you sound even, nimble and controlled.

**The concert pianist**

If you trace out the top line of this piece you'll spot its highest point in bar 5 (B flats). While this isn't an invitation to wade in with a Brahmsian allargando, do use the music's changing landscape to avoid a 'flat', monochrome feel. Experiment with a variety of speeds and dynamics – don't feel hemmed-in by the lack of markings or by the tempo suggestion. Taken too slowly, the sense of line will evaporate (and remember that the virginal had the briefest of note durations), all the delicious contrapuntal detail will lack rhythmic vitality and we may end up relying too heavily on the sustain pedal instead of our fingers. You may wish to modify the ornament at bars 4 and 16.

**Repertoire**

# A Maske

There was no dynamic variation in the keyboard instruments of the Renaissance and Baroque periods, and minimal articulation, which is why there are none to be found in this piece. Add in a variety of dynamics and articulation for your performance.

Giles Farnaby
(1563–1640)

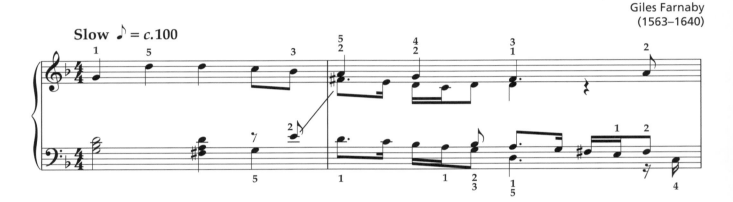

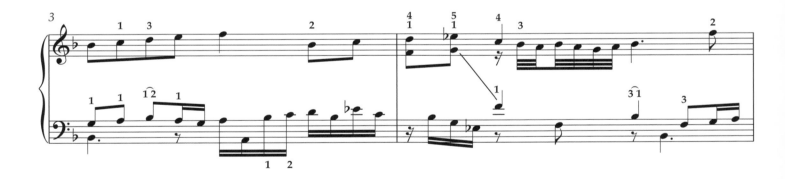

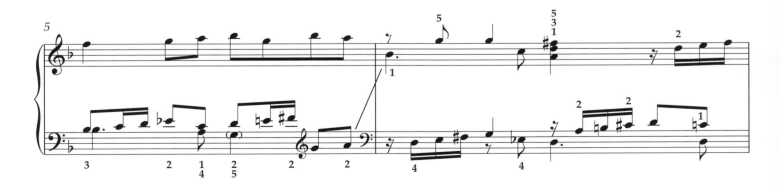

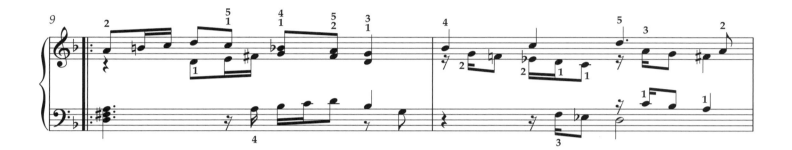

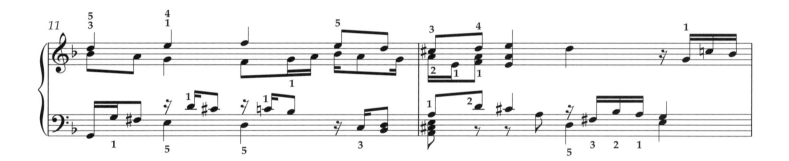

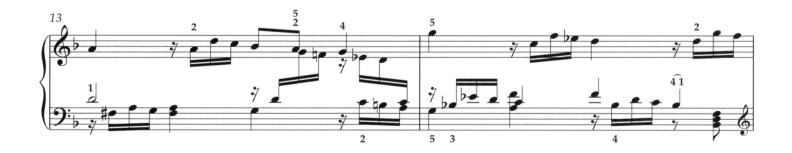

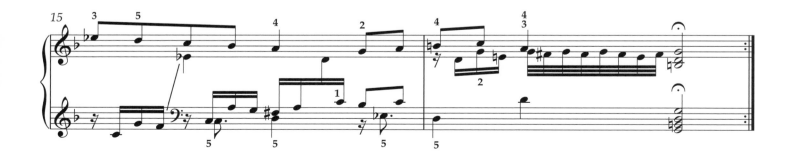

## Dance suites

A Baroque dance suite comprised four dances, all in the same key but with various time signatures. Johann Jakob Froberger (1616–67) is credited with creating the form. For each of the dances listed below, choose the appropriate time signatures and a place of origin.

**Allemande** _____

**Courante** _____

**Sarabande** _____

**Gigue** _____

Spanish     French

$\frac{3}{4}$    $\frac{6}{8}$    $\frac{4}{4}$

German     English

Arguably, the most famous of J.S. Bach's keyboard works are *The Well-Tempered Clavier Books 1 and 2*, however he also composed a great deal of other important keyboard works. Research J.S. Bach's Partitas, French Suites and English Suites and write down some key features.

**Partitas** _____

_____

**French Suites** _____

_____

**English Suites** _____

_____

## Concert pianist

## Parallel 3rds, 6ths and octaves

There are many fingerings for parallel 3rds, though of course the key you are playing in will limit your options. Staccato 3rds, 6ths and octaves on adjacent white keys will often be easiest using the same fingers. But if the upper notes are fingered to give a good legato, you can create the illusion that *both* notes are legato, even when the lower finger has to release its notes early. Practise legato 3rds slowly to listen (and watch) for any asynchronies or bumps. Your hand size will dictate whether 6ths are possible with a fingering other than simply 5 and 1. If not moving too quickly, pianists with a larger stretch can devise legato fingering for some/all of the upper notes, just as with 3rds. Either way, avoid tension gradually building up in the wrist. Where a mix of black and white keys are involved, aim not to wander too far down the keys with flat fingers or you'll limit how even, quick and light they can be. Octaves (and indeed staccato 6ths) can be practised with just the thumb sounding its notes while the 5th finger ghosts its notes above, then reversing: sound the 5th finger's notes while the thumb ghosts.

## Technical gym

Practise these segments, trying out the fingering. Then practise these in both hands and other keys.

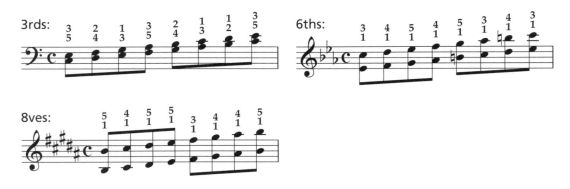

# Russian scales

Russian scales combine similar-motion and contrary-motion scales. Here is a Russian scale for B♭ major and its relative minor, G harmonic minor (the key of the piece on page 10).

## B♭ major

## G harmonic minor

**Activity**

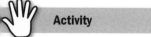

Work out the Russian versions of some major scales and their relative minors. Keep a record of the scales you have studied, below.

**Major scales** _____

_____

**Minor scales** _____

_____

Take a week to explore this piece as a quick study. It is based on the style of Bach's two-part inventions but uses jazz harmony and syncopation. Can you identify any patterns within the music?

# Bach to the Future (A Jazz Invention)

Mark Tanner
(b.1963)

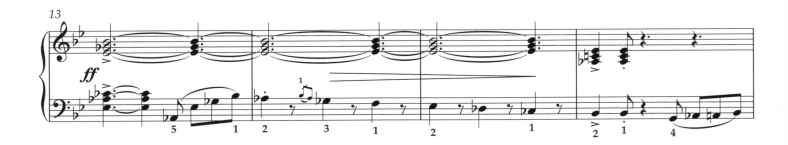

**The concert pianist**

This intriguing rondeau is marked vivement (lively), but this should not be taken as an excuse to hurry. Curiously, the highest note encountered in this piece is G above middle C, and Couperin makes us wait until the second couplet (or verse) even for this brief excursion. Enjoy the cheerful banter between the hands – on a harpsichord this would sound almost hypnotic. The left hand is the music's rudder: let it steer you purposefully – but remain gentle or the music will turn into a kind of Baroque ragtime!

**Repertoire**

# Les barricades mystérieuses

François Couperin
(1668–1733)

# J.S. Bach (1685–1750)

**Baroque timeline**

Corelli 1653–1713

Purcell 1659–1695

Couperin 1668–1733

Vivaldi 1678–1741

JS Bach 1685–1750

Scarlatti 1685–1757

Handel 1685–1759

**Who?** Johann Sebastian Bach was born in Eisenach, Germany, into a family of musicians. He became an orphan at just 10 years old and his eldest brother, Johann Christoph, became his guardian. He was awarded a scholarship to a choir school, where he learnt to play the organ, and composed works for keyboard and organ. Over the course of his career, Bach held many prestigious positions including that of court musician, organist, conductor and Kapellmeister (musical director) for royalty.

Bach married twice and fathered 20 children, with only 10 surviving to adulthood. He is often referred to as a devoted father and teacher.

**What?** Bach's compositional output was vast. The 'Bach-Werke-Verzeichnis', or BWV, lists 1128 works, from keyboard music to cantatas, concertos and oratorios. Some of Bach's most famous works include his *Notebook for Anna Magdalena Bach* (1725) – a collection of pieces written by Bach and some of his students for his second wife, Anna Magdalena. Other works such as *The Well-Tempered Clavier Books 1 and 2*, the *Goldberg Variations*, the *Brandenburg Concertos* and oratorios such as the *Christmas Oratorio*, the *St John* and *St Matthew Passions* remain popular today.

**When?** Bach was born in 1685, in the same year as Handel and Scarlatti. He died in 1750 at the age of 65. He is believed to have suffered a stroke.

**Where?** Bach spent much of his working life in Leipzig. He also worked across Germany including posts in Arnstadt, Mühlhausen, Cöthen and Weimar.

**Activity**

Listen to Bach's *Goldberg Variations* and, if possible, look at a score. What are the technical challenges of performing this music?

_____

_____

_____

**The concert pianist**

When playing Bach, avoid a breathless, unyielding effect by considering where a violinist might lift the bow or a singer would wish to breathe. Wider or more unusual melodic leaps – up or down – could attract extra poignancy/emphasis, but don't linger unduly. Textural definition is usually more than a matter of clear fingerwork – it's about gauging what seems musically most important in the moment, at the same time keeping an eye open for what's next. Playing that is devoid of inflection sounds worse on a piano and does not serve Baroque music well, partly because we are accustomed to hearing a range of effects.

From its characteristic upbeat, this needs to dance. Listen to the Bourrée BWV 996 in E minor for lute/guitar to get a feel for the infectious duple meter. This should skip along enthusiastically, but not so briskly that you skim over the contrasts of articulation that help to bind together Bach's rhythmic detail. Become a cellist in bars 8–14, and from bar 18 the right hand will benefit from the subtlest of dynamic shaping.

**Repertoire**

## Bourrée I from the *English Suites*

J.S. Bach
(1685–1750)

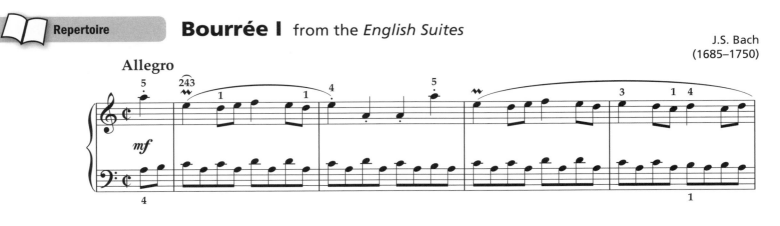

© Copyright 2019 by Faber Music Ltd

# Preludes and fugues

J.S. Bach's *The Well-Tempered Clavier Books 1 and 2* comprise two sets of preludes and fugues in every major and minor key.

What is a prelude? _____

What is a fugue? _____

The following terms describe musical devices used in fugue form. Can you briefly describe each one?

Subject _____

Answer _____

Counter subject _____

Exposition _____

Modulation section _____

Final section (or recapitulation) _____

Stretto _____

Augmentation _____

Diminution _____

Episode _____

Bach's *Well-Tempered Clavier* was such an important work in terms of the way keyboard instruments were tuned. Can you find out why?

This paragraph is about the fugue on page 20. Can you fill in the missing words?

There are _____ voices in this fugue. The subject begins in bar _____ in the right hand. The answer (which is t_____ rather than real) appears in bar _____ in the alto part. The final subject appears in bar _____ in the b_____ part.

Where else can you find the subject and answer in the music? Find them in the different voices and mark them into the score.

Bach's preludes and fugues are the precision engineering of keyboard music. Keep in mind what you've learned about Baroque keyboards, but at the same time explore the effects and qualities you've grown to love on your piano. Don't confuse a lack of expressive markings with a requirement to play inexpressively: rise to the challenge with confidence and insight, and look out for chances to direct the ear to points of interest that occur.

In preludes, always aim to flow, however slow the tempo. In fugues, be active in bringing the individual voices to life; this may mean temporarily subduing other parts of the texture. Wherever possible, coincide where the two thumbs are playing (especially in contrary-motion passages) and when practising hands separately choose fingerings that also work hands together. Legato is often more pleasing than staccato for sustained passages on a piano; search out specific places where staccato notes contrast usefully. Slower speeds often serve Bach better than a hell-for-leather approach on the piano. A more measured speed opens up places where we can be pliable with the rhythms, ornaments and lyrical details, and this is what interpreting is all about.

Answers: 3, 1, tonal, 5, 9, bass

**The concert pianist**

The prelude needs to ripple lightly, with supple arms and wrists; introduce a little more right wrist rotation as you move down the keyboard. Keep left-hand quavers short but not clipped, to encourage shape and musical direction. Rapid exchanges between hands call for extra vitality and finger independence. Be bold with the chords, perhaps adding touches of pedalling to help the declamatory effect.

**Repertoire**

# Prelude and Fugue in B flat major BWV 866/21

J.S. Bach
(1685–1750)

Vivace ♩ = 84

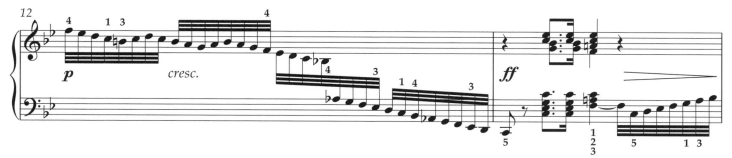

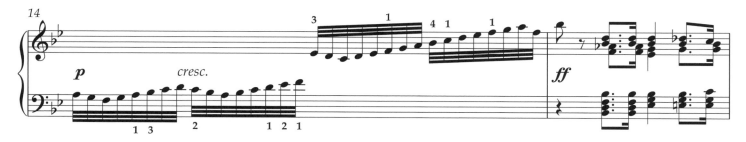

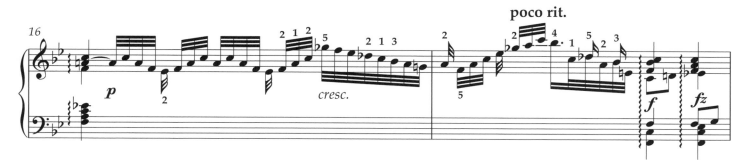

Experiment with various articulations to give this fugue spirit. The triple feel is important, so resist the temptation to scamper away. The ending needs conviction, either with a slight easing-off or a sustained pace and dynamic to give a resounding conclusion.

**Allegro vivace** ♩ = 116
(a 3 voci)

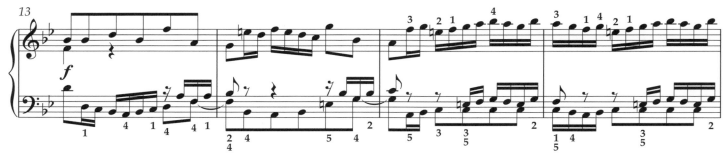

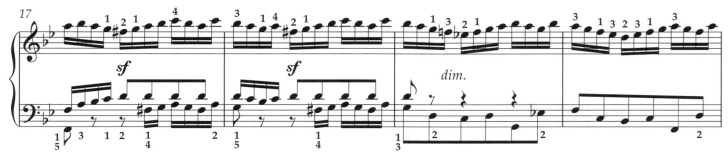

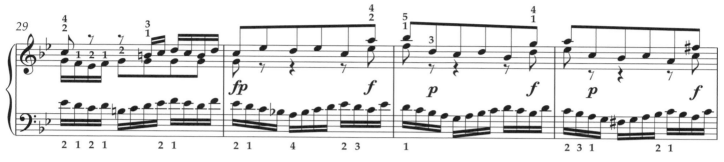

**The concert pianist**

A sarabande is an ancient, slow triple-time dance. Avoid an ungainly thump on the second beats of bars, though a hint of emphasis is characteristic. Broaden the musical landscape as far as you dare, by the end extending to four-bar phrases. Your legato lines should glide, which may require judicious dabs of pedal. The soaring right-hand chords at bars 14–15 almost resemble a lovers' duet.

**Repertoire**

# Sarabande from *French Suite No.1*

J.S. Bach
(1685–1750)

# The Classical period (1750–1820)
## Musical architecture and harmony

**The concert pianist**

## Interpretation

The leather hammers and slick action of the Viennese fortepiano lent itself to nimble passages and decorative articulation. The treble has been likened to a reed, though a device called a moderator could add a wonderful harp-like contrast. The English pianoforte of the same period in contrast had an una corda pedal to the left, a sustain to the right, and greater string tension (though the frame was still wooden) giving a bigger, richer sound. These factors go some way to explaining the contrast of, say, Clementi or Beethoven (pianoforte) and Mozart (fortepiano). Beethoven reveals his fondness for left-hand tremolo and thick chords, emphasis on weak beats and crescendos which drop suddenly. Mozart preferred leaner accompaniments and shimmering running passages and sequences: clarity of texture is paramount.

## Touch and articulation

The rapid note decay characteristic of early Viennese and English instruments suggests the need to play slower pieces a little more quickly. We can also make more of 'sighs' and other articulation-based contrasts. The so-called 'repetition action' that appeared by the end of the period gave greater flexibility for touch and dexterity.

## Phrasing

A compact, symmetrical approach will often work well in Mozart, whereas it may help us to think in larger sweeps when playing Beethoven or Schubert. Expression within phrasing should never be a bolt-on or afterthought: taper off the ends of lines, especially lyrical ones, to achieve a contoured, elegant effect.

## Rhythm and metre

Syncopation is indispensable in Classical music. The rhythmic inflections we take for granted in jazz – delaying a note, 'bouncing' off a bass line or accentuating a weaker note and 'sitting back' on the beat are all foreshadowed in this period, though of course at a more moderate level. Rubato can introduce flexibility to a Classical melody but a 'less is more' approach will serve you well.

## Tone production

Mozart's left-hand parts sometimes include dense low triads that can sound muddy on a modern piano. To compensate, 'voice' a top or bottom note in such chords, or arpeggiate them. We can call upon our instrument's richer tenor region for certain passages, but the thinner tone of Classical instruments is worth keeping in mind, else we paint these delicate strands of music with too broad a brush.

## Use of pedals

An impressive array of pedals existed on fortepianos; sadly, today we no longer celebrate such beautiful effects. Instead we must rely on our ears to decide what sounds effective with our two pedals. The sustain pedal today can hold its bass notes for infinitely longer than players of the day would have been accustomed.

Listen to these works of different genres from the Classical period.
- **Orchestral** Symphony No.22, 'The Philosopher', by Joseph Haydn
- **Chamber or solo** Trio in E♭ KV498, 'Kegelstatt' (for piano, viola and clarinet) by Wolfgang Amadeus Mozart
- **Choral** Haydn's *The Heavens are Telling*, from 'The Creation'

Repertoire from the period recommended for performance or study:
- *Sixty Pieces for Aspiring Players Book 2* by Daniel Gottlob Türk
- Sonatinas by Friedrich Kuhlau, Georg Benda or Anton Diabelli

In the Classical period, ornaments were no longer left to the performer's discretion, but were added to the score by the composer. Here are three studies focusing on three different ornaments. There is also a study in repeated notes and finger changes.

## The trill  Extract from No.36, Op.261

Carl Czerny
(1791–1857)

**The concert pianist**

Above, Czerny is *preparing* you for playing trills with semiquavers, rather than expecting fully fledged ornaments. Aim for evenness and keep the wrist as light as possible as you move from one hand position to the next. Crescendos and diminuendos can be highly effective when playing longer trills, as is starting slowly and building up the speed. Trills should form part of any pianist's technical toolkit. Most right-hand trills work best with 2 and 3 or 1 and 3, but for black-note trills try 2 and 4. Left-hand trills can be slower and may work best with the thumb and 2 or 3. More elaborate fingerings, such as 1323, are worth exploring too, but 'weak' finger trills (3 and 4 or even 4 and 5) are best used only when a composer makes it virtually impossible to use stronger fingers – which is sometimes the case here!

## The acciaccatura  Extract from No.9, Op.88

Hermann Berens
(1826–1880)

**The concert pianist**

The overall speed you play this piece will dictate how brisk the acciaccaturas sound. At very fast speeds the grace note and the 'real' note are almost played together. Don't feel obliged to use the fingerings printed here – at a slower speed, 2 and 3 will serve you admirably throughout, although 4 is more practical in the places indicated if you increase the tempo. Use the minimum finger and wrist movement for playing grace notes – even when practising them slowly. Grace notes add wit to Haydn and charisma to many later styles.

## The turn Extract from No.35, Op.261

Carl Czerny
(1791–1857)

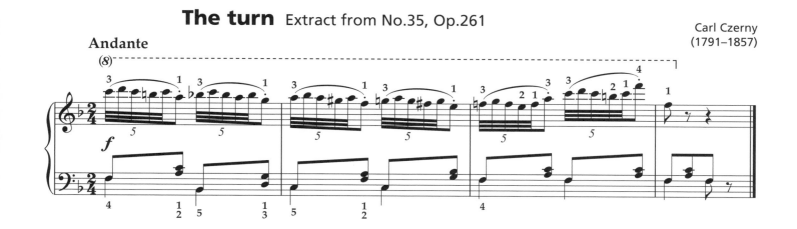

**The concert pianist**

Turns are satisfying to play; though the fingers are doing the bulk of the work, the wrist must play its part, too – a small but decisive down-up motion to coincide with the first and last notes of the turn. A good preparatory exercise can be done on a table: start from just a few inches above and keep a supple wrist as you strike with the thumb: 123451 need to follow suit quickly and evenly so that the second thumb strike initiates an upward motion, leaving you ready to repeat the move. In this exercise we are using 123451 simply to help with feeling even groups of five. Here you are sometimes required to strike with 3 and follow with 43231, so why not adapt the preparatory exercise for this fingering.

## Repeated notes and finger changes

Extract from No.6, Op.100

Henri Bertini
(1798–1876)

**The concert pianist**

Though it's not obligatory (or advisable) to change fingers for all repeated notes, for faster or more extended repetitions we need a reliable technique. The logic is that we avoid having to use the wrist for each note, which leads to slower, heavier, less accurate playing. A useful preparatory exercise is done away from the piano on a table or closed piano lid. A small wrist rotation to the right will help with the first four notes – 4321. Repeat this pattern until it feels dependable, light and effortless, with the smallest input from the wrist. Czerny's pattern, 4321234 (bar 9), will then involve an equally small leftwards wrist rotation after the thumb has played, returning you to where you started.

# Un Poco Andante from Sonata in D, No.6, Op.25

Muzio Clementi
(1752–1832)

**Un poco andante** ♩ = c.72

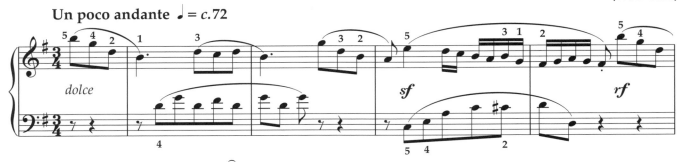

© Copyright 2019 by Faber Music Ltd

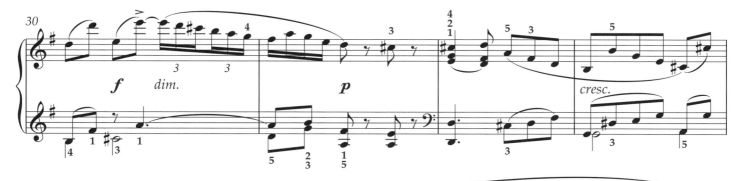

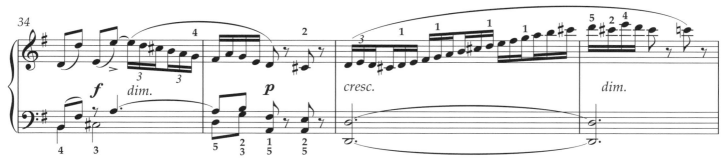

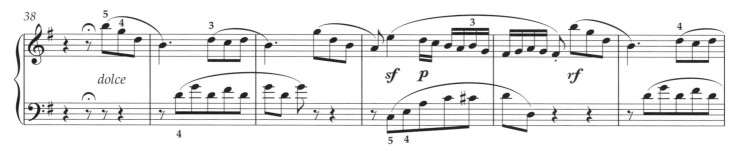

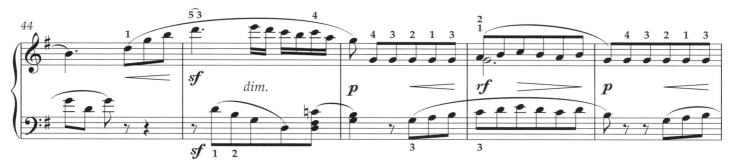

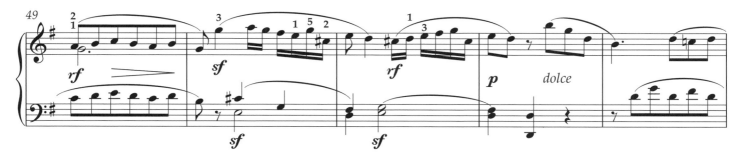

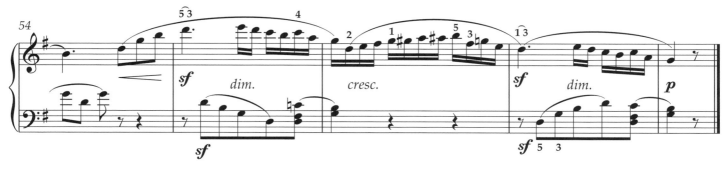

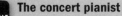
**Chord voicing** You can influence precisely how loud every note sounds within chords. Our default may simply be to use the wrist to affect a downward strike of the keys and let each chord note fend for itself. The trouble is we'll probably hear a flat, one-dimensional effect (and the lower down the keyboard we go, the more important voicing becomes). What's more, there is little prospect of drawing out multiple lines from a string of rich harmonies unless we can control precisely what we hear. Few of us make the piano *sound* orchestral because we are thinking in vertical blocks, not how each block connects musically to its neighbours.

Chord voicing is really an extension of the logic we employ for balancing the hands – but here we are working with the notes played by one hand. Not unlike pedalling, the technique itself is easily learned, but to finesse it takes practice and keen listening skills. Essentially, if we're wanting our chosen note in the chord to sound louder, it will need to travel faster than those surrounding it.

Let's start with a two-note chord, C and E, played with the 2nd and 4th fingers of your right hand. Put the pedal down and begin repeating the chord slowly at a dynamic of *mf*. When ready, make the E sound louder, not by rotating the wrist or 'digging in' with the 4th finger, but by sliding the finger towards you over the top of the key an inch or so as the chord is struck. Once you've got the hang of this, experiment with voicing the lower note, C, by sliding the 2nd finger towards you. You'll love hearing the note ping out. Any asynchrony between the notes should repair itself soon enough – look out through the window and do all this by sound and feel – it's not very visual. Then try three, four or even five-note chords. Don't forget the left hand, and see what sorts of effects you can produce with both hands playing a chordal passage – such as the right-hand rising chords in Mussorgsky's *Promenade*.

**Reading room**

Take a week to explore this quick study. Notice the grace notes, acciaccaturas and arpeggiated chord. Silently play the piece through, identifying the keyboard geography, fingering and hand-crossing. The pedaling is the composer's own; make sure you play it accurately. Use appropriate dynamics to bring out the voice parts.

## Danza de la Rosa

Enrique Granados
(1867–1916)

© Copyright 2019 by Faber Music Ltd

# Sonata form

Joseph Haydn contributed greatly to what we now call Classical sonata form. This structure usually occurs in the first movement of a sonata (a sonata can have up to four movements). Sonata form is comprised of three sections:

**Exposition**: This includes a first subject (or theme) in the tonic key, and a contrasting second subject in a related key. The first and second subjects are often linked by a bridge section.

**Development**: The material of the first or second subject is developed through a variety of related keys.

**Recapitulation**: This repeats the exposition (however it may be varied in some way). Both themes appear in the tonic key and it will often finish with a coda.

| Exposition | | Development | Recapitulation | |
|---|---|---|---|---|
| 1st subject | 2nd subject | | 1st subject | 2nd subject |
| Tonic | Dominant (or relative) | Modulatory | Tonic | Tonic |

**Activities**

Look at the first movement of Mozart's *Sonata in G* on page 34. Can you identify the exposition, development and recapitulation?

Mark in the first and second subjects and their keys.

Can you identify a bridging section between the first and second subjects?

What is the key of the development section? Where does it modulate to?

How has the first subject been modified in the recapitulation?

Go through the movement and identify all the modulations. Mark in cadences as perfect, imperfect, interrupted or plagal.

Beethoven's 32 piano sonatas have been heralded as some of the most important piano works ever written. What can you find out about Beethoven's, Haydn's and Mozart's piano sonatas?

Sonatas are usually in three or four movements. Connect each movement with its typical characteristics, below.

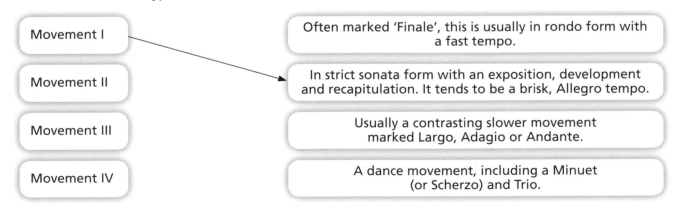

Movement I — Often marked 'Finale', this is usually in rondo form with a fast tempo.

Movement II — In strict sonata form with an exposition, development and recapitulation. It tends to be a brisk, Allegro tempo.

Movement III — Usually a contrasting slower movement marked Largo, Adagio or Andante.

Movement IV — A dance movement, including a Minuet (or Scherzo) and Trio.

Three-movement sonatas typically miss out the dance movement. They will also occasionally include a Theme and Variations as their second movement.

# Wolfgang Amadeus Mozart (1756–1791)

**Who?** Wolfgang Amadeus Mozart was born into a family of musicians. His father Leopold was a competent court musician and his younger sister Nannerl was a talented harpsichord player. They were the only two surviving children of Leopold and Maria's seven children. In 1762, when young Wolfgang was just six, he gave performances in Munich and then Vienna with his father and sister. He continued to tour over the next few years visiting London, Paris, Brussels, Germany and The Hague. By the age of 12 he had composed operas and symphonies, along with many keyboard works. During his career, Mozart worked for a time as a court musician but he struggled to get on with his employers. He enjoyed friendships with Haydn and the Weber family and in 1782 he married Constanze Weber. They had six children, but only two survived into adulthood.

**What?** Mozart's output from his short lifetime was immense, with over 600 works including operas, concertos, symphonies, string quartets, masses and solo piano music. His most famous works include the *Jupiter* Symphony, operas *The Magic Flute* and *The Marriage of Figaro*, chamber music *Eine Kleine Nachtmusik*, his piano sonatas, Requiem Mass, and concertos for clarinet, flute and harp and piano.

**When?** Born in 1756, Mozart died prematurely in 1791 aged 35, leaving Constanze distraught. Having little means and few friends to help out, Mozart was buried in an unmarked pauper's grave, leaving his last work, ironically a Requiem Mass, unfinished.

**Where?** Mozart was born in Salzburg, Austria and died in Vienna. In his lifetime he toured the whole of Europe.

**Activity**

Mozart is said to have had a really mischievous side. What can you find out about the story behind his opera, *The Marriage of Figaro*?

**The concert pianist**

Mozart often gives us model sonatas – themes are clearly 'exposed' in the exposition, then developed before returning with renewed vigour in the recapitulation. Do keep track of this – these are clues as to where we might become more dramatic, or where we should strive for simplicity. Mozart's melodies call for control and craftsmanship. Phrases need proportion, definition and contouring. Running passages should ripple without sounding flustered, impulsive or impeded by pedal. 'Direct' pedal can be applied to good effect in places such as cadences, however, and more rarely in other places such as richly textured slow movements.

There is plenty of charisma to coax out from the pages, even where there is a minimum of dynamics and other markings. Operatic sequences abound in Mozart's more rumbustious finale movements. Elegance (in particular sighs and feminine phrase-endings) is of vital importance when playing Mozart; Alberti bass (as well as more linear) accompaniments need shape and momentum to ensure the lines are carried forward with purpose.

Allow a little space between gestures to help prevent a tense, nervy performance. As a rule keep your fingers close to (and not too far into) the keys and practise the joins between sections to maintain a clear pulse. Stylish rubato is by no means a no-go in Mozart, but we will often achieve the most convincing performance by bringing out sub-melodies and simply following the markings.

Articulation is key, but unlock your dynamic instincts, too; Mozart is often played with an apologetic tone, particularly when coupled with a sluggish pace. My pianist of choice for Mozart is Murray Perahia; he adds the emotional content without compromising its crystalline beauty.

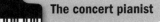

**The concert pianist**

You may be familiar with CPE Bach's *Solfeggietto* in C minor, a popular toccata-style workout. Mozart's *Solfeggio* is an Adagio with a suave, chromatic melody. In Bach's piece only one note is played at a time, with groups passed rapidly between hands, while in Mozart's not a single chord appears in either hand – it's almost an exercise in frugal writing in which Mozart doffs his hat to the masters of counterpoint. Enjoy the moments of repose, such as bars 8, 9 and 11, and when the oboe-like triplets first appear, from bar 15, let them trickle from your fingers using your best legato.

**Repertoire**

# Solfeggio in F  KV.393 No.2

Wolfgang Amadeus Mozart
(1756–1791)

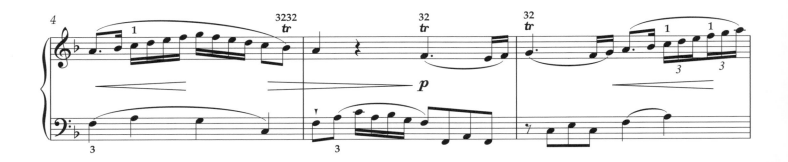

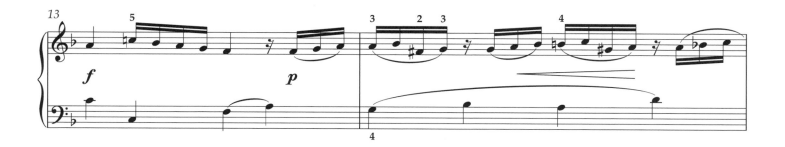

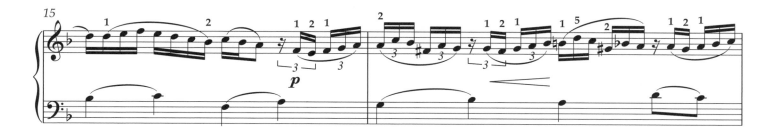

**The concert pianist**

Sonata in G (page 34): keep the triple feel intact throughout – not easy when accents occur on the third beats, such as bars 30–33 and 97–100. We must guard against acceleration, prime examples being bars 16–22 and 31–53. Hands separate practice can help you to retain an easy musical flow while negotiating the music's many shifts in register and dynamics – begin practising as an elegant minuet and increase the speed gradually. An 'orchestral' effect occurs at bar 75 that should sound unexpected and dramatic.

# Sonata in G K283

Wolfgang Amadeus Mozart
(1756–1791)

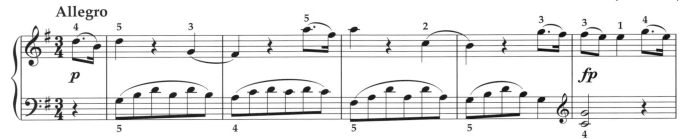

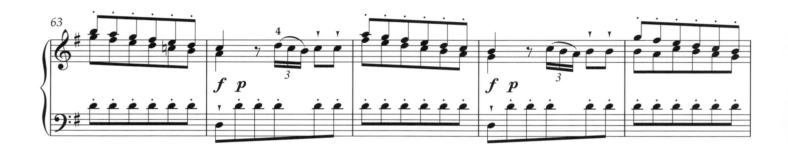

# Figured bass and the $\frac{6}{4}$ chord

**Figured bass** is a type of notation often found in Baroque scores in which numbers and symbols are used to indicate intervals and chords. The numbers indicate the intervals above the bass note. Can you fill in the blanks in the following figurations?

For further details see *The Intermediate Pianist* Book 3 page 41.

$\frac{5}{3}$ = root position

$\frac{6}{3}$ = _____ inversion

$\frac{6}{4}$ = _____ inversion

7 = _____

Where no number is given it is assumed to be a $\frac{5}{3}$ (root position) chord. $\frac{5}{3}$ is only written when a chromatic note is included or it is part of a $\frac{6}{4}$, $\frac{5}{3}$ chord progression.

- The **cadential** $\frac{6}{4}$ is used to approach chord V at a cadence: it has the same bass note.

- The **passing** $\frac{6}{4}$ is used to allow the bassline to move in step, usually from the tonic to the mediant (third) or vice versa, using chords **I Vc Ib** or **Ib Vc I** as shown below.

Complete the following exercise in 4 parts, which includes a passing $\frac{6}{4}$ and cadential $\frac{6}{4}$. This is called realising the figured bass. Remember, if there is no number, it is a $\frac{5}{3}$ (root position) chord. A good way to tackle this is to write a chord grid for the key (see *The Advanced Pianist* book 1 page 22) and write the chord and inversion underneath each bass note (as given below for the first two chords), before filling in the notes.

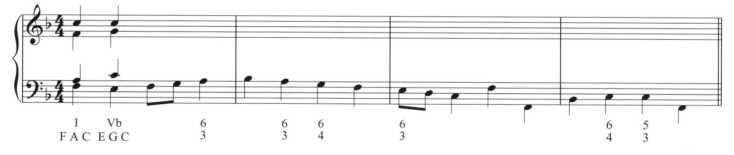

# Chromatic harmony: common chords

- The **diminished 7th** is a 4-note chord made up of minor 3rd intervals.

- The **Neapolitan 6th** chord is a first inversion of a flattened chord II (the supertonic) – the root and 5th are lowered a semitone. So in C major, chord II (D, F, A) becomes F, A♭, D♭.

- **Augmented 6th** chords include an augmented 6th interval between the bass and an upper part, are built on a flattened sixth chord and usually precede chord V. There are three different types, each containing a different note (shown below, in C major, in the soprano part). The **Italian** chord contains the tonic, the **French** the 2nd degree of the scale, and the **German** the flattened 3rd.

Mark in the augmented 6th interval in these examples. Can you write your own Italian augmented 6th in a different key in the blank stave above? Remember it will need to resolve onto chord V.

**The concert pianist**

## Keyboard overview
This period saw radical improvements in the capabilities of fortepianos (produced in Vienna) and pianofortes (produced in London) – a wider range (during Beethoven's life increasing to 6 octaves) and an una corda pedal that allowed one string to be struck instead of three. Until this point, the harpsichord had possessed an unbeatable capacity for volume compared to its percussion-powered rivals – but this was set to change once and for all; the turn of the 19th century would bring impressive advances in tone quality and quantity.

## Touch and articulation
Much of the lightness and clarity you would instinctively bring to Mozart, Haydn or early Beethoven will serve you well in Schubert and late Beethoven, since by today's standards articulation was still the main variable. You can begin to consider a more adventurous dynamic range, however. A little more upper body power will bring authority and intensity to fortissimo climaxes.

## Phrasing
Keep in mind that these instruments had a shorter sustain compared with what we take for granted today. Phrasing needs to be balanced and you will notice a move towards longer, more chromatic cantabile lines.

## Rhythm and metre
Richer harmonies and accompaniments require us to establish a discernible pulse to avoid a soupy mix which undermines the music's rhythmic impulse. The musical machinery is there to help propel it forwards, however, not to impose a mechanical approach. Bear in mind we are still only at the threshold of the Romantic era, hence our rubato will sound most effective in moderation.

## Tone production
Melodies feature with increased prominence in the middle register, and although these would not have had the resonance and projection of a later instrument, we should use our best judgement to gauge how best to balance the hands and chords. While the dynamic range of Schubert's or Beethoven's instruments were far narrower than on a modern grand, do explore the subtle shades in between, which leaves plenty of scope for cantabile shaping.

## Use of pedal
It's easy to swamp this repertoire with sustain pedal, so apply a little-and-often approach to ensure harmonies register clearly. On larger instruments in particular we may need to half-pedal more frequently in order to flush out middle/treble notes but retain some bass sonority.

Recommended repertoire:
- Beethoven's Sonata Op.110 – the Adagio movement offers excellent practice for expressive cantabile playing.
- *Practical Exercises for Beginners* Op.599 by Carl Czerny
- *Waltz in A* by Carl Maria von Weber

Listen to these works of different genres:
**Orchestral** Trumpet Concerto in E major by Johann Nepomuk Hummel
**Chamber or solo** *Death and the Maiden* by Franz Schubert
**Vocal** Franz Schubert's Lieder

# Chromatic scales

Chromatic runs are common in piano repertoire, so should be practised in different ways. You will also encounter chromatic scales a 3rd and 6th apart and in double thirds in a wide range of pieces. Add these to your practice routine and try them with various dynamics and articulation:

Chromatic scale a 3rd (or 10th) apart, similar motion:

Chromatic scale a 6th apart, contrary motion:

Chromatic scale in double 3rds, similar motion:

Take great care with these scales to make the best legato possible. This is achieved through a combination of acute listening and good fingering choices; finger control will be helped by keeping close to the keyboard.

**The concert pianist**

The word 'chromatic' refers to colour, and in pianistic terms this simply means the full spectrum of tones and semitones available to us. The black keys become an obstacle course if you allow your fingers to wander too far into the keys.

Fast chromatic passages became increasingly commonplace at this time – a splendid example is the descending flourish used by Beethoven to transition from the Grave to the Allegro in the *Pathétique* Sonata. Chromatics are best executed with the fingers in a 'C' curve, keeping as supple as possible – avoid seesawing the wrist or bearing down on the keys if you want your chromatic to sound dramatic!

# The Ghost in the Chimney

Explore chromatic scales in the right and left hand in this extract.

Theodor Kullak
(1818–1882)

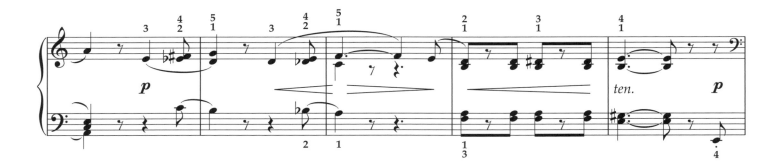

Take a week to study this piece. Its challenges include hand-crossing, accidentals, articulation, dynamics and pedalling. Look out for any patterns.

## Andantino Op.46

Stephen Heller
(1813–1888)

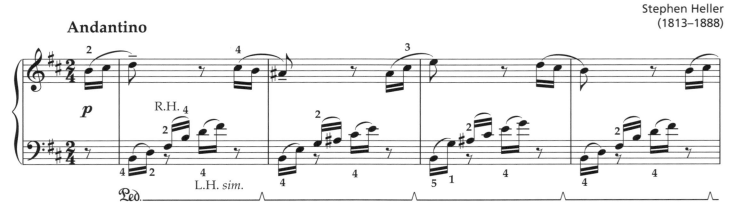

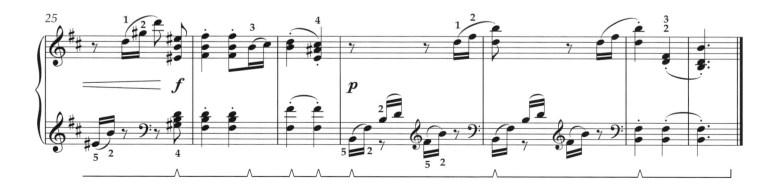

# To Alexis

Hummel was a pupil of Mozart. This piece is late Classical or early Romantic, and is from his comprehensive piano tutor, *Klavierschule*.

Johann Nepomuk Hummel
(1778–1837)

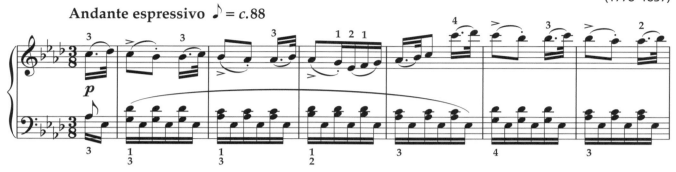

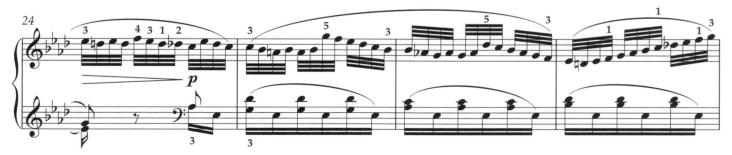

The phrasing and fingering are from Hummel's original piano method.

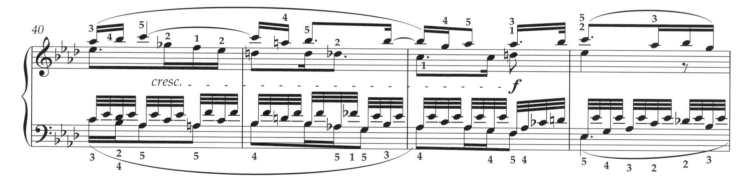

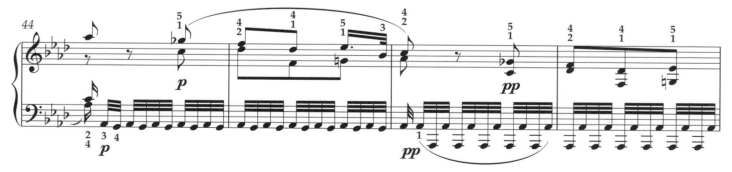

# Practising scales

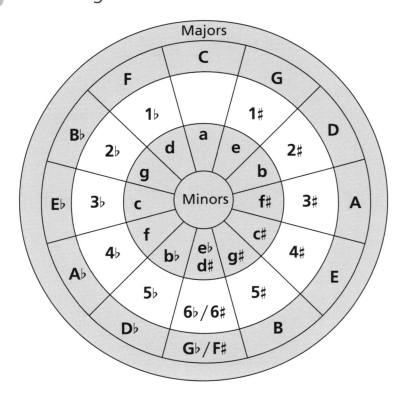

The **circle of 5ths** is a useful tool to help structure how you learn and practise scales. Take related segments of the circle, perhaps the major and its relative minor, or a scale and its neighboring segments, for example.

Remember to try scales in contrary motion, and a 3rd and 6th apart as well.

**Activities**

In the circle of 5ths select a segment or two for your practice each day. Are there any you don't know that you can try? Play them with different articulation (legato/staccato and different articulation in each hand), dynamics and rhythms (dotted).

Here is a table of fingering groups for all the major and minor scales (giving the starting positions). Knowing scales in finger groups can help with memorising and practising. The first group has been filled in for you. Can you add in the remaining scales in the correct fingering groups?

**Scales to include:** Majors  F   B (LH)   F♯   B♭   E♭   A♭   D♭

Minors  B (LH)   F♯   C♯   G♯   F (RH)   B♭   E♭

This is not a comprehensive list but a useful starting point. Perhaps there are other patterns that occur to you?

| Group 1 | RH 123 1234<br>LH 54321 321 | C major, G major, D major, A major, E major, A minor, E minor, D minor, G minor, C minor, LH only F major, F minor, RH only B major, B minor. |
|---------|------------------------------|-------------------------------------------------------------------------------------------------------------------------------------------------|
| Group 2 | RH 231<br>LH 321 | |
| Group 3 | RH 21<br>LH 21 | |
| Group 4 | RH 234<br>LH 432 | |
| Group 5 | RH 1234 | |

# Ludwig van Beethoven (1770–1827)

**Who?** Beethoven was born in Bonn, Germany. He left school at 11 and later went to work and study with court organist, Christian Gottlob Neefe. Beethoven held positions at the Bonn Opera and Court whilst also working as an instrumental teacher. He moved to Vienna in 1792 where he performed regularly and studied composition with Haydn. He was a virtuoso pianist and played the viola, violin and organ. He never married or had children, and for the last 25 years of his life suffered from hearing loss. He is viewed by many to be one of the greatest composers of all time.

**What?** Beethoven composed 32 piano sonatas, five piano concertos, nine symphonies, an opera and a large amount of chamber music, including string quartets. He is said to have written in three periods, the first being Classical (up to 1802), influenced by the work of Mozart and Haydn. The middle period is from 1803–1814 and demonstrates more Romantic compositional ideas. The final period, from 1815 to his death, produced arguably some of the greatest works of his career.

**When?** Beethoven composed during the Classical and early Romantic periods, dying of liver disease in 1827 at the age of 56.

**Where?** Beethoven was born in Germany, but spent a significant period of his life living in Vienna, Austria.

**Bridge timeline**

Dussek 1760–1812

Beethoven 1770–1827

Hummel 1778–1837

Weber 1786–1826

Czerny 1791–1857

Schubert 1797–1828

## The concert pianist

Beethoven's piano music can all too easily sound bombastic. Put such caricatures to one side and enter the nuanced sound world of a composer whose inner ear went at least some way to compensating for his tragic loss of hearing. Pianists could usefully bring some of our digital Mozartian technique to our Beethoven playing (and perhaps a little of our Beethovenian charisma to our Mozart playing). There are more than a few foretastes of impressionism to enjoy in Beethoven's writing, especially in the later piano music, but even here pedalling calls for our most sensitive application.

We often need to bring additional muscularity to the outer movements of Beethoven's sonatas, especially when presented with extended tremolos, arpeggios and 'moto perpetuo' type passagework. However, fatigue quickly sets in if we dig deep into the keys or work too hard in flourishes which rely more on evenness and shapeliness for their success.

Rhythmic emphasis, syncopations and *fp*/*sfp* moments require a varied array of touches – from your nimblest staccatissimo to your weightiest tenuto. Cultivate a 'cellist's' cantabile for Beethoven's more ruminative minor key music. Celebrate chances to be light or even jovial when basking in a sunny major key.

Think 'big', as opposed to 'loud' in climaxes, and keep in mind the lighter action of Beethoven's instrument if you find yourself struggling to meet an unrealistic tempo. Beethoven's string quartet style can bring an unexpected Classical grandeur, especially perhaps to his later writing, where clarity of texture and a beady eye for score markings will transport your interpretation to another level.

## Activity

Beethoven was a master of harmony. In Bagatelle No.11 and the first movement of the sonata, find examples of the following and fill in their bar numbers. (See page 39 for an explanation.)

1 Diminished 7th _____

2 Dominant 7th _____

3 Cadential $\frac{6}{4}$ _____

Suggested answers: Dim. 7th: Bagatelle No.11, bar 8, 3rd beat, LH. Dom. 7th: Bagatelle No.11, bar 22, 2nd beat. Cadential $\frac{6}{4}$: Sonata in A major, bars 91–92.

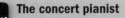 

Even right-hand quavers will set you up well in this Bagatelle – do try out alternative fingerings, e.g. 142512425; whichever you settle on, be sure to cover as many notes as you can in each hand position, as though you'd been asked to play block chords. You'll find your wrist glides rather than jerks, and you'll play fewer wrong notes, too. The left-hand's oom-pah-pah accompaniment should dance; a gentle emphasis on the first beats will help you. At bars 8 and 20 you can practise the 'subito piano' – these should sound dramatic but not exaggerated.

**Repertoire**

# Bagatelle  No.9, Op.119

Ludwig van Beethoven
(1770–1827)

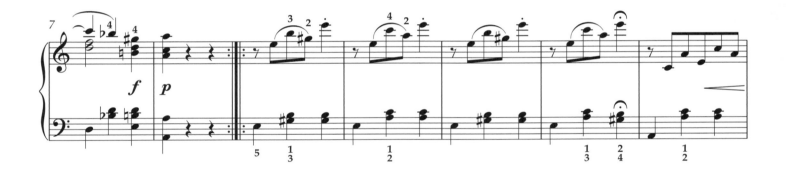

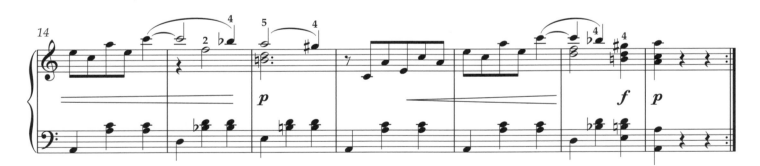

© Copyright 2019 by Faber Music Ltd

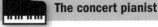 **The concert pianist**

Imagine the next Bagatelle played by a string quartet, especially its first part, which leads to a diminished seventh at bar 8 that is loaded with anticipation. Your legato playing will be tested in both hands – see how well you can achieve this without pedal at first, especially at bars 19-22, which also invite your most contoured phrasing. In bars 10-18 your balance will need real sensitivity; the left hand is like pizzicato strings under a soaring first violin cantabile line. Overall, this Bagatelle calls for a poetic yet measured approach.

# Bagatelle No.11, Op.119

Ludwig van Beethoven
(1770–1827)

**Andante, ma non troppo**

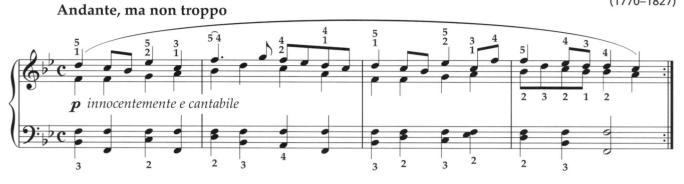

*p innocentemente e cantabile*

*cresc.*     *p*   *dim.*

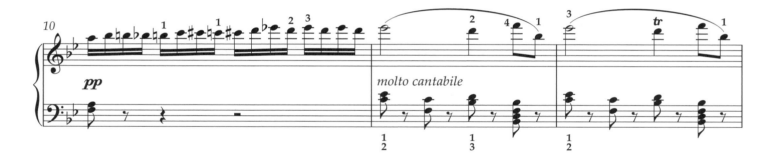

*pp*     *molto cantabile*

*p*

*tr*
13

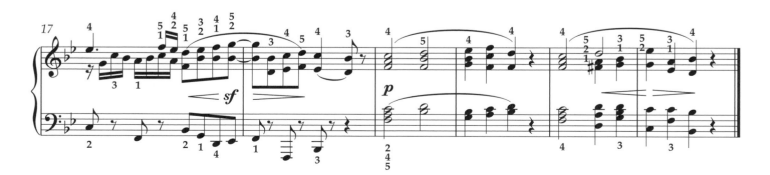

*sf*     *p*

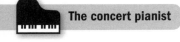
**The concert pianist**

Practise the right hand as though it is legato, choosing fingerings to minimise hand shifts. Enjoy an almost reggae effect with your left hand off-beats, which need full note lengths, and avoid over-emphasising the thumb notes.

**Repertoire**

# Bagatelle No.10 Op.119

Ludwig van Beethoven
(1770–1827)

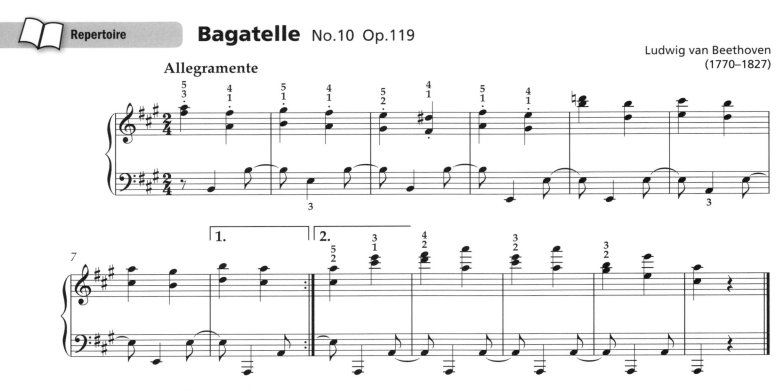

**The concert pianist**

This sonata perfectly sums up Beethoven's late style: approach it with imagination and an eye for detail. Don't be intimidated by its poetical design or darker moments. Think lyrically rather than how you might impress an audience technically. Break up thicker chords or if necessary leave out a note or two.

**Repertoire**

# First movement from Sonata in A major No.28, Op.101

Ludwig van Beethoven
(1770–1827)

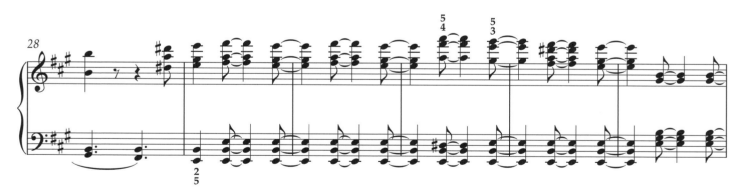

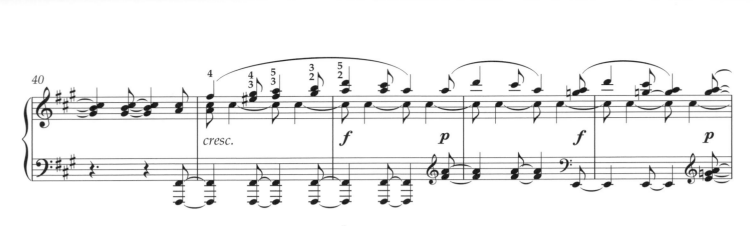

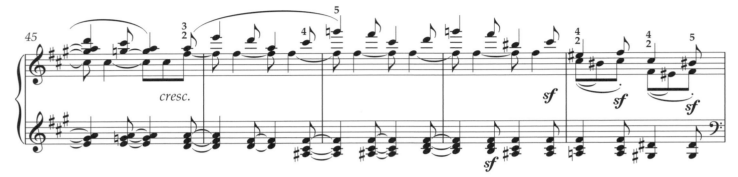

* Brackets indicate suggestion to split large chords in two for smaller hands.

# 4  The Romantic Period
## Storytelling, picture painting and orchestral piano playing

 **The concert pianist**

## Keyboard overview
By around 1860 the piano as we know it had been fully developed, including the sostenuto (middle) pedal: the music of late Brahms and Liszt would have sounded pretty close to what we hear today. This does mean that the music of the early Romantics (Chopin, Schubert and Schumann) was largely composed in a transitional period, moving from wooden to iron construction, which would add to the piano's tone, dynamics and duration.

## Touch and articulation
Accents and tenutos (often combined) tend to be almost as ubiquitous as staccato/legato, and non-legato markings are also frequently seen. Different articulations can be found within the notes of one hand, and a whole range of touches become common, from the bel canto, operatic cantabile to leggiero (a gossamer-like touch favoured by Mendelssohn and others). In combination with a vastly expanded dynamic range, the effects achievable were seemingly boundless.

## Phrasing
The relatively compact 'speech-like' phrases of the 18th century gave way to more ambitious, free-flowing piano-centric lines: symmetry and balance were no longer necessarily the benchmark for a well-composed melody. The move towards richer harmonies, climaxes and passages of heightened intensity also had a stretching-out effect on melodic lines.

## Rhythm and metre
Romantic rubato was by now a more liberally applied aspect of personal expression. Tempo adjustments crop up in various guises, along with copious character indications. When coupled with the wealth of dynamics and articulation indications already mentioned, the scores take on a decidedly busy appearance when compared with earlier works.

## Tone production
A resonant bass, singing tenor and bright treble are aspects of modern pianos we take for granted, but do bear in mind that it took over a century and a half of progression, not to mention a lengthy power struggle between the fortepiano, pianoforte and harpsichord. Latterly, it was the Industrial Revolution which made possible a more powerful, consistent instrument with a wide range of notes.

## Pedals
Romantic harmonies and textures simply could not work without an efficient sustain pedal. More than this, the pedal became invaluable for adding sonority and ambience. In its infancy the pedal had been more of a colouristic tool, and yet ironically on the modern piano there are times when its capacity to sustain can appear almost too efficient. This has required pianists to evolve a range of compensating techniques, among them half-pedalling and quarter-pedalling.

## Recommended repertoire
Rachmaninov's Prelude in D Op.23 No.4, Chopin's *Raindrop* Prelude in D flat No.15, waltzes and intermezzos by Johannes Brahms, *Consolations* by Franz Liszt.

Listen to these works of different genres from the Romantic period:
- **Orchestral** *Symphonie Fantastique* by Hector Berlioz
- **Chamber or solo** Octet in E♭ by Felix Mendelssohn
- **Vocal** *La Traviata* by Giuseppe Verdi

# Promenade

Take a week to explore this quick study. Mussorgsky was part of a group of important Romantic Russian composers known as 'The Five'. This piece is taken from his famous work, *Pictures at an Exhibition*.

Notice the change in time signatures. It may help to identify and write in the names of the chords.

What can you find out about the 10 pieces Mussorgsky wrote in *Pictures at an Exhibition*?

_____

_____

How many pieces in the collection are called 'Promenade' like this one, and why do they keep appearing?

_____

_____

Modest Mussorgsky
(1839–1881)

**Moderato commodo assai e con delicatezza** ♩ = 104

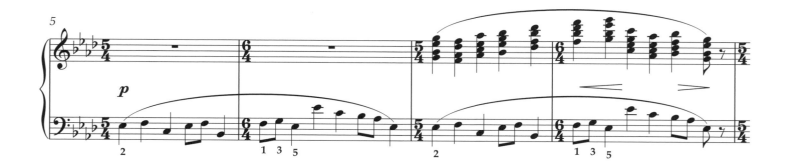

**Exploring cross-rhythms** Cross-rhythms occur when two different rhythms are played simultaneously. First work out which notes sound together and then where the other notes sound in relation. Be confident of the notation before you begin, and aim for a flowing rendition.

**The concert pianist**

Cross-rhythms, or polyrhythms, are where the hands are at cross purposes. The subdivisions of the main beat might be duplets in one hand and triplets in the other; this is by far the most common scenario you'll come across, though fours against threes are also common. You might wonder why composers do this. There are a variety of valid reasons, including a) wanting a more interesting texture, b) giving the melody a clearer definition over an accompaniment and c) wanting to make one hand more pianistic, even if this means creating a co-ordinational difficulty.

- First try to make sense of cross-rhythms by doing some basic arithmetic. This works well for threes-against-twos, producing the well-known 'nice cuppa tea' rhythm. However, arithmetic isn't so convenient for other rhythms: fours-against-threes becomes 1.33 recurring! For this reason we're usually better off learning the passage in question by feel, having perhaps sketched in a few vertical pencil lines as visual aids.

- Cross-rhythms, interestingly, are often easier to play faster, as in Chopin's *Fantasie Impromptu*, perhaps because we then add natural emphasis to the first of each group, which are places we can be confident always coincide. Eventually, we'll need to airbrush out these accents so that each part lives its own distinctive life.

- Table-tapping can help in the initial stages – take fours-against-threes: allocate three moving fingers to one hand and four to the other, 123 in the left and 1234 in the right. In contrary motion, coincide the thumbs and let the remaining fingers follow suit in their own good time. Focus first on what one hand is doing (tap louder), then switch around. As long as the thumbs coincide, don't concern yourself with arithmetic! Eight-against-five sounds preposterous, yet if you tap out an imaginary scale of C in your right hand (one octave, continually looping back) and simultaneously tap 12345 in your left (not calculating but *feeling* them), you'll soon have your thumbs matching confidently enough to switch the hands around, or try more unusual finger patterns.

# Extract from *Duo Sentimental*

from *Miniatures* Op.52

3 against 2

Joaquin Turina Pérez
(1882–1949)

# Extract from No.89, Op.261

4 against 3

Carl Czerny
(1791–1857)

# Lento No.90, Op.261

8 against 3

Carl Czerny
(1791–1857)

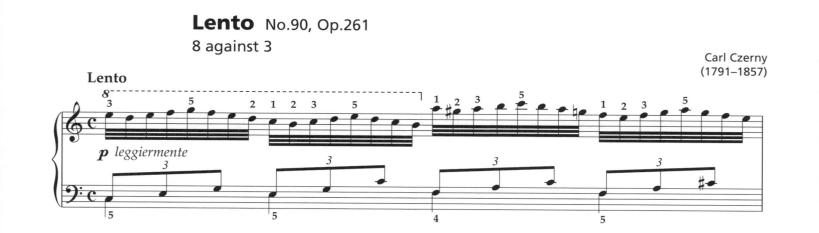

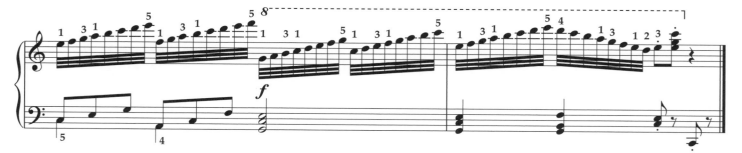

For this *Duetto* to resemble a duet, the melody needs a different character from the bass. The harmonic shape has been skilfully judged – it's like a piece of musical elastic, stretching and relaxing, but never fully at rest. At the heart of a convincing performance will be your ability to coax a tune from the thick texture, with touches of pedal to sidestep any unstylish blurring. A leggiero touch will serve you well.

**Repertoire**

# Duetto No.6, Op.38

Felix Mendelssohn
(1809–1847)

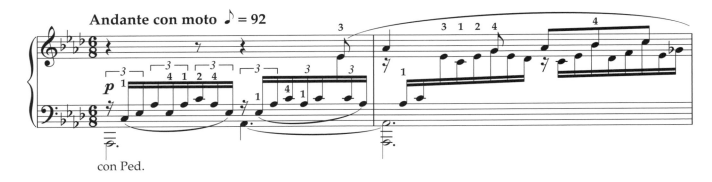

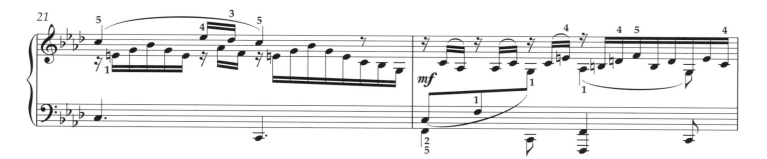

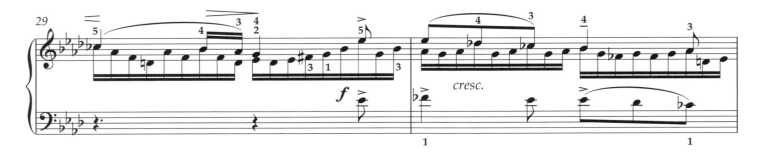

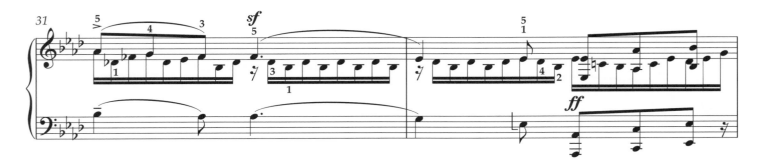

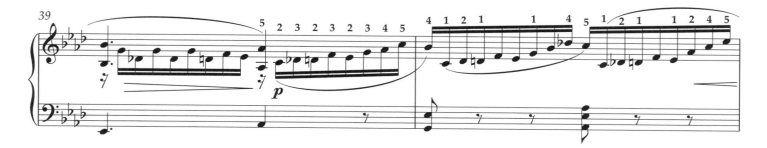

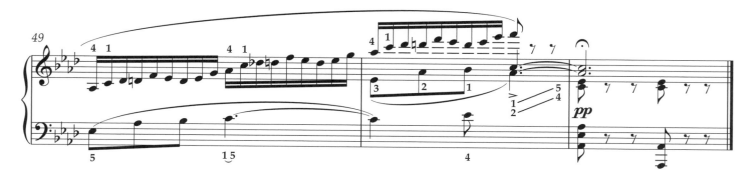

# Frédéric Chopin (1810–1849)

**Who?** Chopin was born to a Polish mother and French father. He had his first music published when he was just seven years old (Polonaise in G), and he regularly performed in public in Warsaw from the age of eight. His parents ensured young Frédéric received an excellent education, first at the Warsaw Lyceum and later at the Warsaw Conservatoire, majoring in composition. Chopin spent his career performing, teaching and composing in high society across Europe. He had a number of romantic interests including the author George Sand (pen name for Amantine Dupin) and Maria Wodzińska, and had friendships with Mendelssohn, Berlioz and Liszt.

**What?** Chopin wrote a prolific number of works for the piano. He composed ballades, études, impromptus, mazurkas, nocturnes, polonaises, preludes, rondos, scherzi, sonatas, variations, waltzes, fantasies and other miscellaneous pieces for piano. He also composed two piano concertos, chamber music and songs. The influence of Nationalism can often be heard in his music.

**When?** Chopin died in 1849, aged just 39, due to ongoing health issues with his lungs.

**Where?** Chopin was born in Poland but left at the age of 20, moving to Vienna and then on to Paris. Apart from a short spell in Majorca (with George Sand) and England he remained in Paris until his death in 1849.

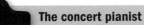

**Activity**

What can you find out about Chopin's preludes?

_____

_____

_____

**The concert pianist**

- Chopin's piano music represents the vast bulk of his compositional output. A vocally conceived melody lies at the heart of his music, perhaps best epitomised in the nocturnes. A sense of dance is just as important, however, in the waltzes, mazurkas and polonaises.

- Virtuosity, though abundant in the scherzos, ballades and sonatas, should never be seen as a goal in itself – even in the études there is invariably a melodic line that lodges itself in the memory. *Fiorituras*, those mysterious looking filigree 'cadenzas' in small print, are a trademark feature that can soak up hours of practice in order to sound feathery and spontaneous.

- Much is made of rubato in Chopin's music, but the idea that we precisely 'repay' any time borrowed from one bar or phrase in the next is virtually impossible in practice, not to mention undesirable. What matters is that the melody and harmony make sense without sounding calculated or retrofitted.

- Pedalling is another area where we can easily become unstuck. Be mindful of where the harmonies are moving towards (and which specific notes/lines seem to be tugging the harmony somewhere new) then our foot should have little difficulty in adding valuably to the effect.

- The preludes are an excellent place to start – they are short enough to be approachable, stylistically very representative, and yet each is perfectly crafted.

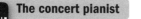

**The concert pianist**

The 'sostenuto' direction is a clue to the music's sedate pace and sustained, silky-smooth legato – feel an unhurried triple time right from the anacrusis. Notice phrase marks, which vary between two and six bars. The left hand has a wonderfully contoured melody in the second half – don't allow the grace notes to distract you from the important rhythmic flow here – careful touches of pedal will prevent a bumpy ride. Bar 15 is probably the trickiest spot, though a combination of methodical fingering, deft pedalling and the poco rit. should ease this most perfect of perfect cadences.

**Repertoire**

## Waltz in E♭ KK IVb No.10

Frédéric Chopin
(1810–1849)

**The concert pianist**

It is rare to hear the opening four bars played convincingly. Done well, the listener is left with an air of expectation – spend time perfecting this deceptively simple 'string quartet' texture. Bars 15, 49 and 53 are notorious: unfold the right-hand notes in long, soaring gestures. The transitions between triplet quavers and triplet semiquavers could sound like a gradually tumbling snowball. Elsewhere, hands separate practice will ingrain the accompaniment and encourage a chocolatey-smooth finish. At bars 58-61 keep close to the keys and do it all with the fingers.

**Repertoire**

# Nocturne in C♯ minor Op. posth.

Frédéric Chopin
(1810–1849)

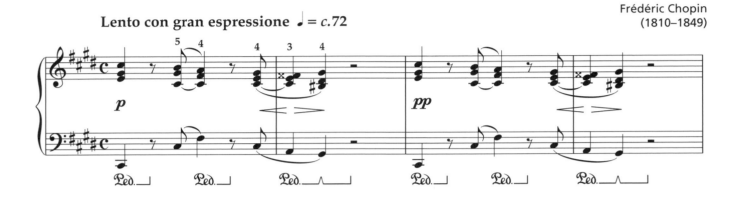

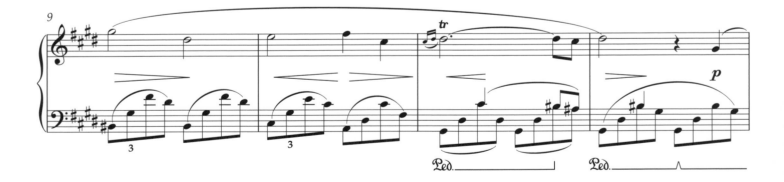

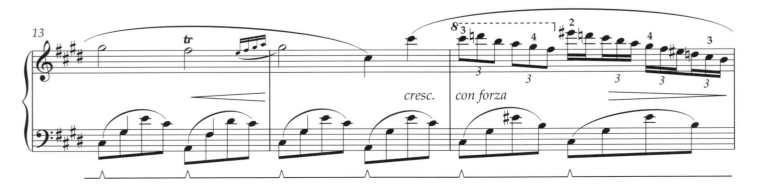

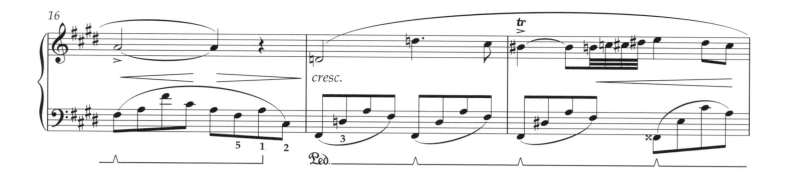

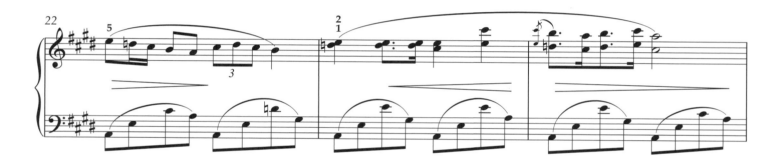

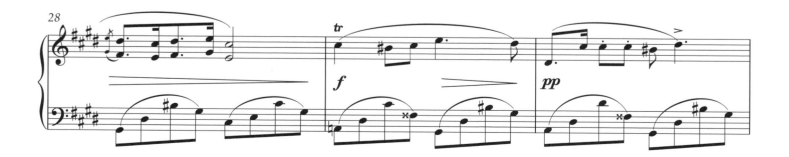

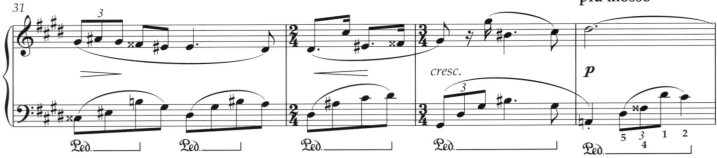

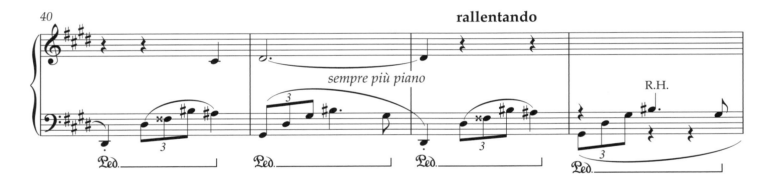

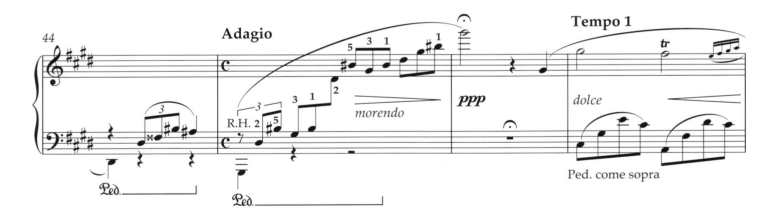

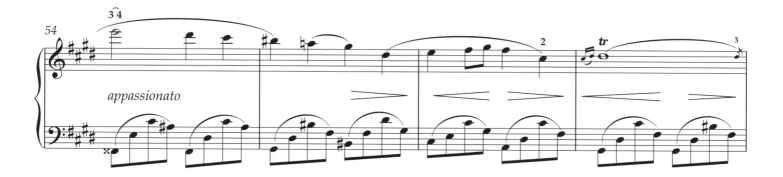

# Nálada No.139, Op.41

Zdeněk Fibich
(1850–1900)

**Lento** ♩. = 40
*molto cantabile*

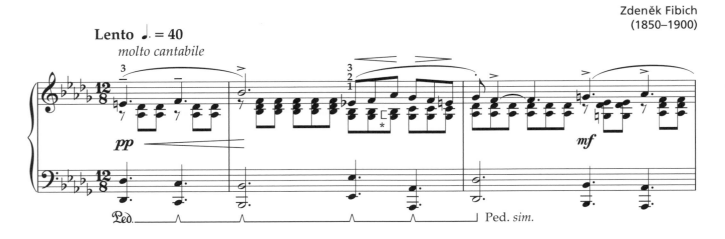

* denotes chord can be split.

© Copyright 2019 by Faber Music Ltd

# The basics of jazz

Beethoven was a master of harmony, structure and improvisation. Here, concert pianist Mark Tanner discusses how these elements have evolved and are used in jazz today.

- **Structure** Jazz often starts with a simple statement of the tune, known as the 'head' (section A). The repeated chord shape of the head's accompaniment is used as the basis for improvisation in the B section, which is usually eight bars long and called the 'middle 8'. This is followed by a reprise of the A section, which might be a little shorter. A brief coda gives the music a sense of finality. This AABA structure is a jazz variant of ternary form.

- **Harmony** Jazz uses many harmonic devices from the Classical tradition, such as chords I, II, IV, V and VI, and cadences to give closure to phrases. Adding notes 2, 6 or 7 to a major triad gives a jazzy effect (D, A or B added to a C major triad). Experiment with these chords, trying them in different keys.

- **Jazz scales** Whole-tone scales and diminished scales are often used in jazz:

  *Whole-tone scales*: each note is equally spaced a tone apart creating an atmospheric sound, especially with the sustain pedal.

  *Half-diminished scales* form a pattern of a semitone followed by tone: C, C♯, D♯, E, F♯, G, A, A♯. This scale, and the diminished chord on which it is based (C, D♯, F♯, A), works well when used together with a dominant 7th chord.

- **Rhythm** The rhythms and accents of Classical music centre on the first and third beats of the bar. The syncopated rhythms of jazz music often make a feature of notes accented on the second and fourth beats. Dotted rhythms are used, in which the short notes are 'leaned' on more than the long ones.

## Activities

Play the half-diminished scale on C in your right hand over a $C^7$ chord (C, E, G, B♭) in your left.

Can you spot a half-diminished scale in the next piece?

Play a half-diminished scale with a dotted rhythm emphasising the notes given in bold: **C**, C♯, **D♯**, E, **F♯**, G, **A**, A♯. Now try it the other way around.

Go through the whole piece and identify three or four interesting chords. What do they sound like when played together in a chain? If they don't make musical sense, try reordering them, or replace one for something else. Then try improvising using this new mini progression.

Transpose the scale at bars 9–10 up or down a tone or two, and then experiment to find which chords sound effective with it in the left hand. You could make up an entire piece by moving from one scale to the next, or by going up one scale and then down another.

---

### *At First Light* improvisation tips

- **A little goes a long way** The stemless notes in the solo section (bars 13–16) show the possibilities for improvising over the left-hand chords. Don't feel you have to be 'busy' to be effective.

- **Be adventurous with the keyboard** Don't feel locked into the middle of the piano – experiment with higher notes. Try combining two or more notes to make interesting chords.

- **Get locked in** Make sure your left hand is able to repeat its chord sequence without conscious effort. Then gradually add notes, perhaps tucking these in between the chords rather than playing them with the chord.

 **Activity**    Prepare your own improvisation for bars 14–16.

# At First Light

Mark Tanner
(b.1963)

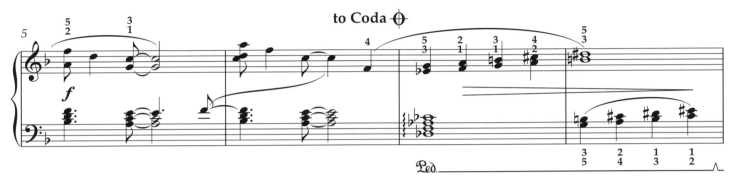

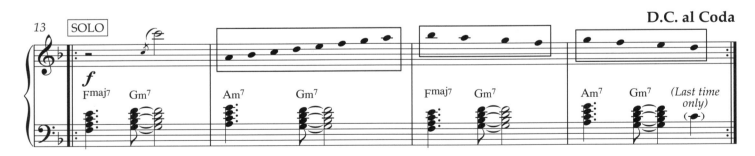

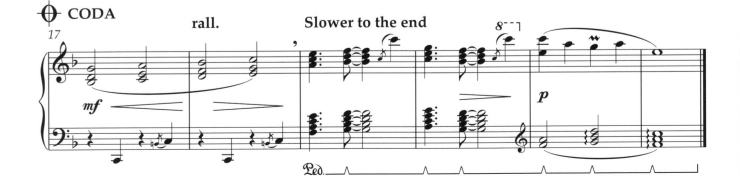

 **The concert pianist**

## Touch and articulation

The double-escape action invented by Érard at the beginning of the 20th century added immensely to the possibilities at the pianist's disposal. We take for granted an ability to return hammers back to their strings well before gravity has returned them to their resting positions, but without this device the impressive repeated notes we admire in contemporary repertoire would be virtually impossible.

## Phrasing

Thankfully, the crafting of a good melody has remained a key skill for many contemporary composers, even when faced with the opposing traffic of atonalism, serialism, impressionism and minimalism. Interestingly, throughout all this, Rachmaninov remained a tunesmith par excellence, whose endless melodies call for our most insightful shaping, balancing and voicing.

## Rhythm and metre

A glance at scores by Bartók, Prokofiev or Stravinsky will reveal irregular rhythms and numerous changes of time signature. For these composers the confounding of a pulse seems to have been a gateway to expression. All three instinctively grasped the relationship between rhythmic inflection, emphasis and articulation. Jazz rhythms such as syncopation inevitably became fused with less conventional time signatures to form the complex hybrid styles specific to Adams, Adès, Brubeck, Kapustin and countless others. In all cases a decisive tempo is key to keeping these rhythms meaningful and intact.

## Tone production

It was perhaps inevitable that experimental piano music would emerge at some stage. John Cage's 'prepared piano' pieces required objects to be positioned between or directly on the strings. It is perhaps surprising that there have been relatively few extensions of Cage's revolutionary approach since the 1930s. Most contemporary composers have chosen to work with the instrument in the form they inherited it, or have been enticed in different directions – electronic, sampled or synthesised sound sculptures.

## Pedals

Most pianists neglect the sostenuto pedal; it is the piano's best-kept secret. Used in combination with the other two, it can open up an intriguing universe of effects. Experiment with the middle pedal whenever you find yourself struggling with music written on three staves or in multiple textures, also in pieces such as Debussy's *La cathédrale engloutie* or Rachmaninov's Prelude in C♯ minor, where bass pedal notes need sustaining while upper harmonies require regular flushing out. You can even use it in earlier 19th-century music in places; it is simply another tool to effective piano playing.

Recommended repertoire from the period:
* Baines's *The Chimes* and Messiaen's *La Colombe* (The Dove)
* *Night Pieces* by Peter Sculthorpe
* *The Cat and the Mouse* by Aaron Copland

Listen to these works of different genres from the period.
* **Orchestral** *The Rite of Spring* by Igor Stravinksy
* **Chamber or solo** *Praeludium and Allegro* (for solo violin) by Fritz Kreisler
* **Choral** *Lux Aurumque* (Light and Gold) by Eric Whitacre

## Pedalling

Although we have just one sustain pedal there are countless ways of using it. Many players are a little lazy with their right foot, reaching for it as a default response whenever the hands play together, or in place of fingering that could accomplish the task more cleanly. Actually, the sustain pedal holds a universe of subtle effects which stem naturally from the repertoire we are playing. Examples include direct pedalling to achieve selected moments of colour, such as at cadences in Classical (or even Baroque) pieces; or as a tool to stir together grander harmonies typical of those we encounter in the Romantic period. Alternatively, it can create beautiful, ambient effects which remind us of Debussy (or perhaps go further still into the realm of Birtwistle and Takemitsu). But even this is a crude survey of the valuable uses to which we might put the humble right pedal. Like the accelerator in a car, it's not just 'up' or 'down' – there are shades in between, as well as ways of flicking it part way to help convince the ear that a perfect transition of harmonies has just taken place.

Listening skills are invaluable when it comes to the 'black art' of pedalling – no amount of deft footwork will help us if we are not the most attentive member of our audience! Pianists tend to practise in a small space and perform in a larger one, so it's worth bearing in mind that a boomier room will do some of the pedalling for you. As a general rule, don't reserve pedal for the places indicated in scores, and don't use it just because it says to! The piano you are playing on, the acoustic it's in, the speed and dynamic you are playing at are all factors that affect when, where, how and whether to use it.

**Activities**

- Play a slow ascending legato scale (no pedal), one octave in the middle of the keyboard, using the fingering you're used to.

- Play it again, so that the overall effect sounds identical, but this time using one finger and the sustain pedal. Touch your ear with the same finger in between playing each note and use your best legato pedalling.

- Play a deep octave of the scale's key note, *ff*, 'trapping' it with the sustain pedal. Next, at a dynamic of *pp*, play the same scale as before with one finger, but this time try half-pedal (a decisive half-flick of the foot) after every note you play. Done well, you should still be able to hear the bass note lingering on, but with fairly clear legato scale notes. Depending on your piano and how the pedal is regulated, you may only be able to achieve this for the first few notes of the scale.

## Fingering tips

1 Always test out your fingering up to tempo – there's no point in fingerings which only work at the slow speed you adopted when practising.

2 When mulling over which fingers to use, try to minimise shifts in hand position; practise these as cluster chords to check they really work. Too many thumb-shifts will inevitably make for a bumpy ride.

3 Use strong fingers wherever possible – your 3rd finger is especially versatile, not just in scalic or arpeggio patterns, but for stretching large intervals, making awkward leaps, joining up legato octaves/chords and making a 'singing' sound.

4 Think outside the box. If you have small hands, consider taking a note or two in the other hand, trapping a bass note with the pedal, playing two notes with one finger/thumb, arpeggiating unstretchable chords or simply missing out a note that isn't essential to the musical flow.

5 When working out how best to play tricky running passages in both hands, try to coincide both thumbs (or another finger); doing this aids memorising and gives a physical as well as visual guide. Try to come up with a fingering that will also work if the music reappears in different keys later on.

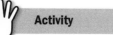

**Activity**

Bartók's pedalling is shown in the score. What do you notice about it? Can you mark in some appropriate fingering?

**Technical gym**

# Melody in the Mist

Béla Bartók
(1881–1945)

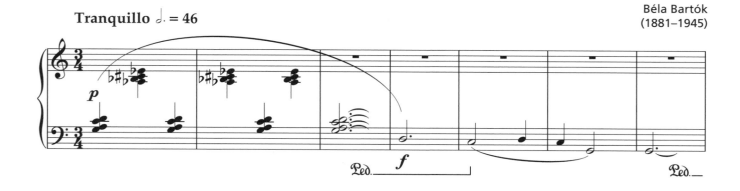

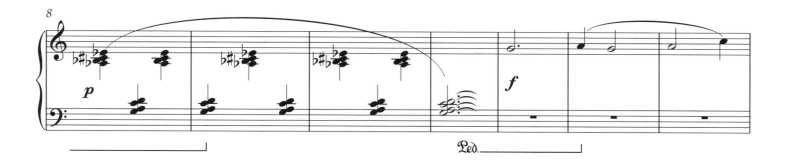

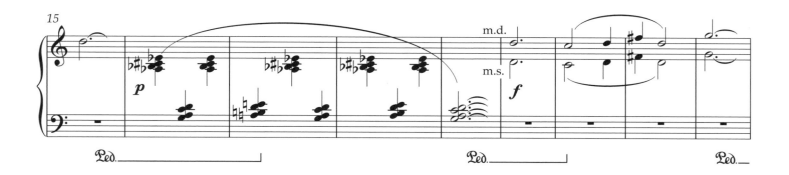

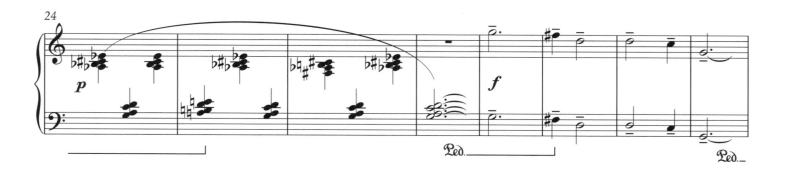

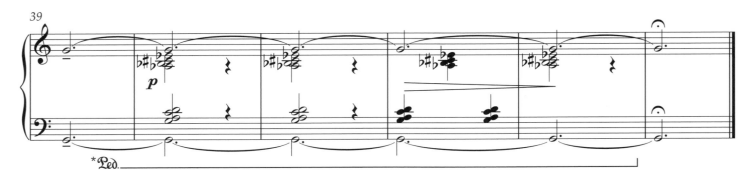

\* use the sostenuto pedal here if possible. If not, use the sustaining pedal as marked,
replacing your fingers silently on the G's before releasing the pedal.

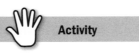 **Activity**

Mark in the pedalling (damper and una corda) and fingering on the score of
*Sound Waves*. Pedal with the harmony. Swap fingers on repeated notes, and use
traditional fingering patterns for arpeggio-type runs.

**Technical gym**

# Sound Waves

Karen Marshall
(b.1971)

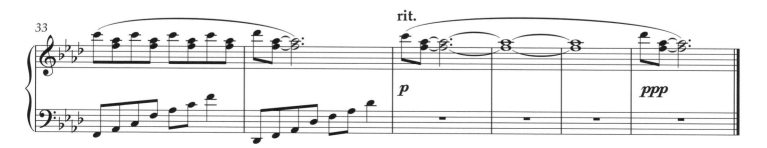

**Musicianship**

# Improvisation

Use these melodic motifs by great composers to improvise eight-bar melodies. Think about what scales you could use. Try to include melodic devices like sequences, inversions or even retrograde melodies.

Invention No.8 by J.S. Bach

Sonata in D by Haydn

*Of Foreign Lands and People* by Schumann

*In the Mist* by Janáček

Improvise or compose an accompaniment for the melody using the chords below. The start of the accompaniment has been provided to help you.

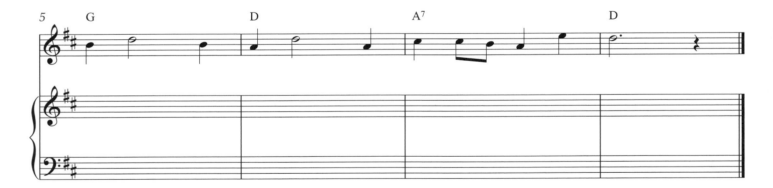

**The concert pianist**

Prelude: In just 24 bars Scriabin takes us on an action-packed journey in which the left hand retains the tune: you'll want it to sound full, resonant and purposeful. Scriabin's choice of $\frac{6}{4}$ is significant – it's as though he is trying to stretch out time itself. Try playing sections of it at double or even triple speed, then revert to your slow tempo to see if you can still just about feel two beats per bar. Hands separate practice will pay dividends – we're after the smoothest of melodies and a 'cotton-wool' right-hand accompaniment. (See page 28 for more on chord voicing.) Intriguingly, the loudest dynamic marking is just *mf* (bar 8), and even this is over soon – most of the piece is *p* or *pp*.

# Prelude No.4, Op.11

Alexander Scriabin
(1871–1915)

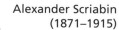

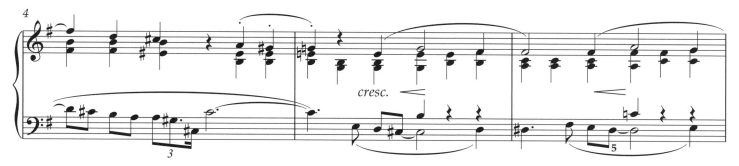

Take a week to study this piece by Satie. Notice the tied notes, the interesting harmony and the lack of bar lines. Check the accidentals carefully.

## Danse de Travers No.2

Erik Satie
(1866–1925)

*Passer*
Go on

*Pareillement*
Likewise

*Du coin de la main*
With the corner of the hand

*Seul*
Alone

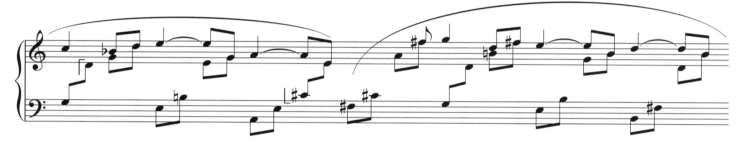

*Être visible un moment*
To be visible for a moment

*Sa raccorder*
To get together again

*Un peu cuit*
A little intoxicated

# Sacro-Monte No.5
## from *Cinco danzas gitanas* Op.55

Joaquín Turina
(1882–1949)

**Allegro moderato** ♩ = *c.*88

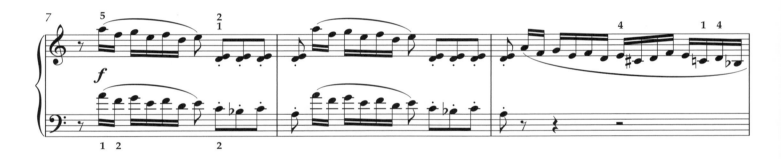

**Più vivo**

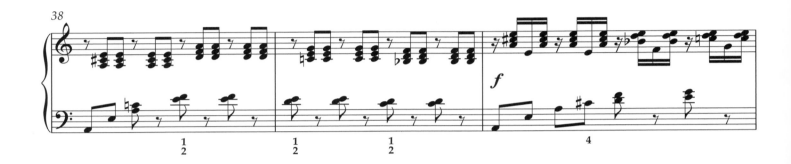

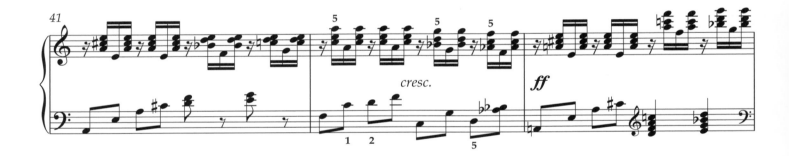

**The concert pianist**

*Sacro-Monte* is one of those pieces you'll want to keep under your fingers for an off-the-cuff concert. Its rhythms need to fizz with vitality; much of its impact comes from sudden unannounced outbursts, rather like fireworks, so don't be caught napping! Spend lots of your practice time working on the connecting tissue, such as from bar 6 to 7, etc. A likely trouble-spot worth sorting out is bars 12–14; memorise the leaps here from the unison notes down to the chords and back.

# Claude Debussy (1862–1918)

**Who?** Debussy was born in Saint-Germain-en-Laye, near Paris. His parents were not particularly musical or wealthy but Debussy's godparents paid for him to have piano lessons. He gained a scholarship to the Paris Conservatoire aged 10. Debussy failed to develop as a piano virtuoso but became increasingly successful as a composer, winning the Prix de Rome. He had a very colourful private life, marrying twice. He had one child, who he adored, Claude-Emma Debussy, who died just a year after her father. He was a friend of the composer, Stravinsky.

**What?** Claude Debussy composed nearly 200 works including those for orchestra, piano solos and duets, chamber music, operas and other vocal music.

**When?** Debussy lived at the end of the Romantic period and beginning of the 20th century. He is often described as an 'impressionist' composer (although he disliked the term), and his work was influenced by the art and literature of the time. Born in 1862, he died of cancer aged 55.

**Where?** Debussy was born in France but also lived in Germany, Russia and England. He was particularly fond of England, and completed *La Mer* whilst living in Eastbourne. It was also where his daughter was born. He died in Paris.

**Activity**

What can you find out about Debussy's *Children's Corner*? What inspired him to write these pieces?

**Concert pianist**

Alhough Debussy rejected the Impressionist label, it's not hard to see why it stuck. In particular, the evocation of nature – water, light, snow, etc. – is exquisitely captured. His music often has an air of a moment in time expertly caught on camera. Unlike music from the Romantic period that immediately preceded it, there generally isn't that sense of personal journeying, heroism, passion or motion towards a climax. Debussy can appear lightly perfumed one moment, extravagant the next. Our task as pianists is to move convincingly from one mood to the next, presenting the most exotic, vivid imagery we can.

- Sustain pedal is crucial when playing Debussy, although we are mostly left to decide where and when to use it. Resist the idea that we can simply drench everything with pedal – we need to hear where the harmonies, textures and registers change.

- Whole-tone and pentatonic scales, gamelan effects, parallel or modal harmonies and 'added' notes are all typical of Debussy's language. But his music is far more inventive than a list of common features. Look beyond the obvious traits to unlock a magical sound world for you and your listeners.

- Spend time on voicing and balance – Debussy's piano writing can sound one-dimensional unless we tease out inner lines and secondary melodies.

- Don't overlook Debussy's subtle articulation and dynamics, or places where una corda or sostenuto pedals could help. He has many ways of telling us to be expressive or flexible.

- Rhythmic precision is important – Debussy's music needs to be fluid, as if on a magic carpet. Some pianists feel there is a specific Debussy touch that underplays the percussive aspect to give a shimmering effect. The key to this is to listen with absolute concentration.

**The concert pianist**

There are over a dozen tempo indications in the score, which shows how precisely Debussy built in the rubato. Though pedal is usually indispensable in Debussy, these pieces have no markings to assist us. Sometimes the briefest of dabs will suffice on the second beats (such as bars 5–13), but you can be more generous elsewhere (bars 13–18). Enjoy the hemiolas at bars 19–20 and the lovely 'viola' line bars 21–30.

**Repertoire**

# Page d'album

Claude Debussy
(1862–1918)

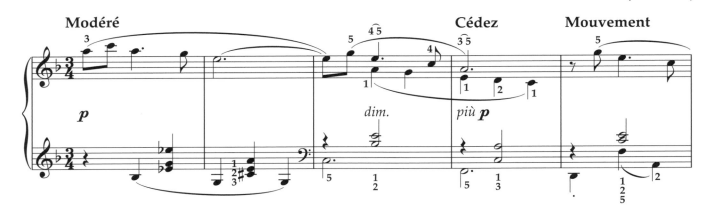

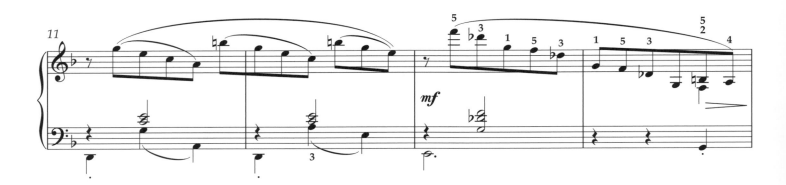

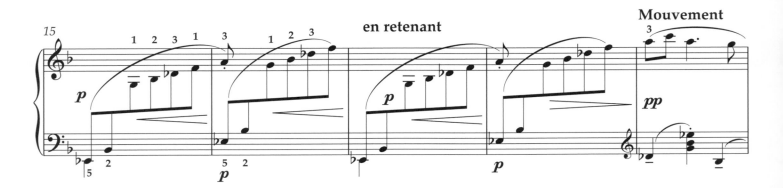

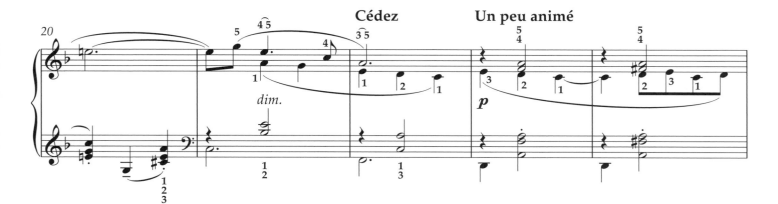

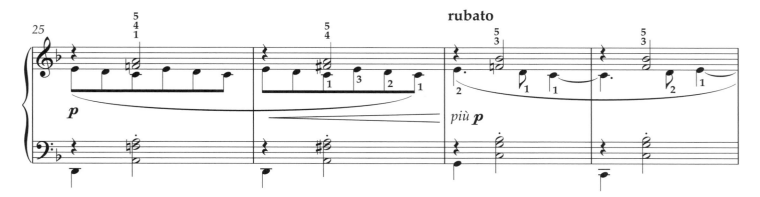

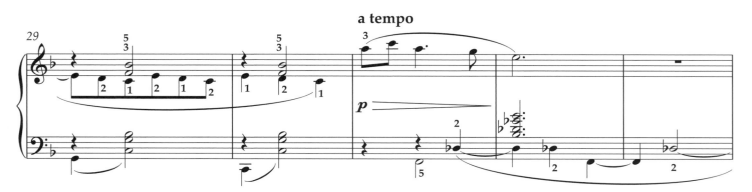

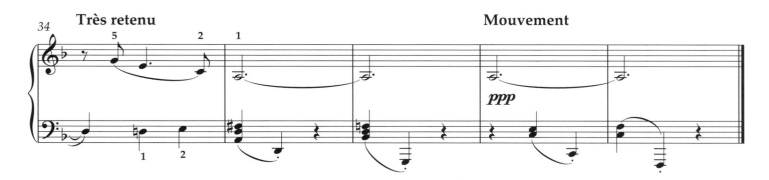

**The concert pianist**

The subtitle of the next piece translates as "To invoke Pan, god of the summer wind". A pastoral sounding 'flute' melody needs practising in isolation, but many areas will only feel coherent when rehearsed together. Once the time-signature changes have been thoroughly learnt, try to ignore them: the musical flow is what's key. Attention to the French terminology is non-negotiable – look up anything you don't know. Explore Debussy's colour scheme, do add ideas of your own and be in no hurry to move between musical gestures.

# Pour invoquer Pan, dieu du vent d'été

from *Epigraphes Antiques*

Claude Debussy
(1862–1918)

Modéré – dans le style d'une pastorale ♩ = 80

Un peu plus mouvementé

En retenant

© Copyright 2019 by Faber Music Ltd

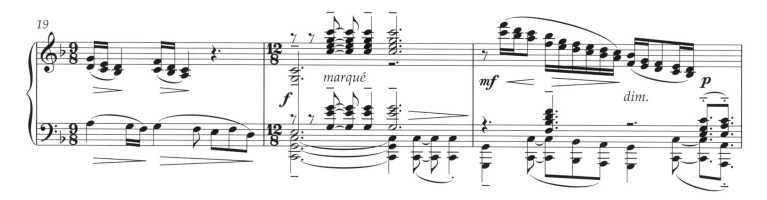

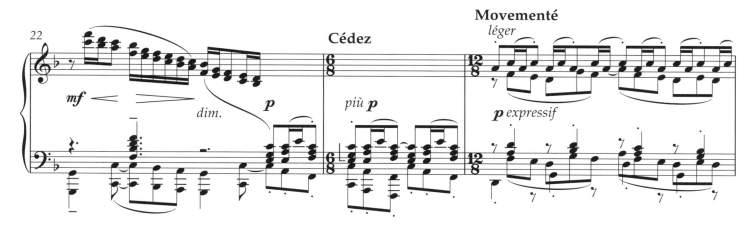

# Mindfulness and the piano

Mindfulness has enjoyed something of a revival in more recent times, though let's not forget its ancient Buddhist origins. Mindfulness should not be something 'other people' do; indeed its broader message should chime with musicians because we are asking a lot of ourselves when we practise for long periods, let alone perform to others.

At the heart of mindfulness is self-compassion – being alive to what's going on around you without letting it intrude on your inner calm, not over-reaching or 'end-gaming' but enjoying the process of improvement. It's also about being purposeful yet realistic about what you are doing, and placing the musical experience at the top of what is important. Achieving a 'flow-state', whereby you and your piano no longer seem like separate entities is surely something all players can aspire to.

For the vast majority of pianists, piano playing is a leisure activity. Even if you plan to study music at a higher level, ultimately it'll be your ability to communicate something of lasting musical value (or compose or write about music, teach it or use it in some other way) that will make your efforts seem worthwhile. This does not mean that the casual pianist is merely filling in time or playing just for 'entertainment'; done mindfully, piano playing should complement the other things you do in your life, and elevate its power to engage, inspire and move others. Each time you sit down to play, let it take you to a place inside yourself away from the noise and stress of daily life.

**Activities**

- Write down a dozen 'mindful piano challenges' on slips of paper or flash cards. They need to be very specific, but only a few words long (be realistic – make each small but achievable). Examples could be a tricky thumb transition in a scale or an unusual rhythmic snippet, chord pairing or ornament in a piece you are working on. Pull out a card at random when you feel your practice is becoming frustrating. Set aside five minutes and work with concentration on it. Enjoy feeling completely immersed in the challenge, pausing to reflect whenever you want. You're not after perfection, just improvement: remember that learning is a journey, never a destination.

- Take a long, deep breath. Close your eyes and play the most beautiful, slowly descending scale as you breathe out through your nose. Listen intently so that the volume of each new note begins at precisely the level the previous note had reached. This perfect decrescendo should flow with your exhalation, so your breathing *is* your scale. You may find you run out of breath as the last note decays to *ppppppp*. A couple of octaves could take you perhaps 30 seconds …

Also available:

The Mindful Pianist
Focus, practise, perform, engage
Mark Tanner

“ Its fresh approach is both invigorating and thought-provoking … I wholeheartedly recommend it to pianists of all levels. ”
*Martino Tirimo*